52 LOVE

WEEKLY LOVE LESSONS IN BITE-SIZED BITS

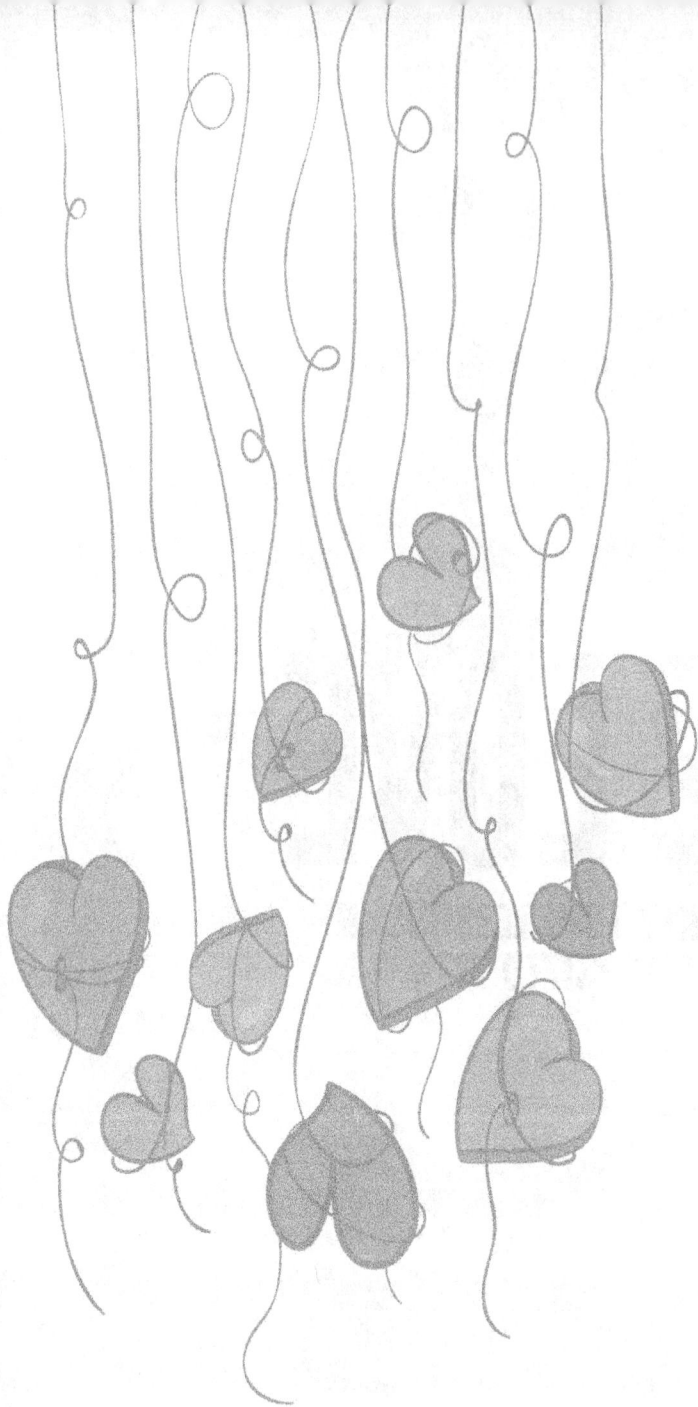

52 LOVE

WEEKLY LOVE LESSONS IN BITE-SIZED BITS

Tonya Todd

Accomplishing
Innovation Press

4 Horsemen
Publications, Inc.

Accomplishing
Innovation Press

Published By: Accomplishing Innovation Press an imprint of 4 Horsemen Publications, Inc.

Accomplishing Innovation Press
℅ 4 Horsemen Publications, Inc.
PO Box 419
Sylva, NC 28779
4horsemenpublications.com
info@4horsemenpublications.com

Chapter Art and Illustrations by Lauren Jones
Cover Design by Autumn Skye
Typesetting by Valerie Willis
Edited by Laura Mita

Library of Congress Control Number: 2023940205

Paperback ISBN-13: 979-8-8232-0244-2
Hardcover ISBN-13: 979-8-8232-0246-6
Audiobook ISBN-13: 979-8-8232-0243-5
Ebook ISBN-13: 979-8-8232-0245-9

To Charles, Diamond, and especially Lucian Blake for inspiring so many of the suggestions in this book.

"Special dedication and so on to all lifestyles, sizes, shapes and forms."

~ Beastie Boys

TABLE OF CONTENTS

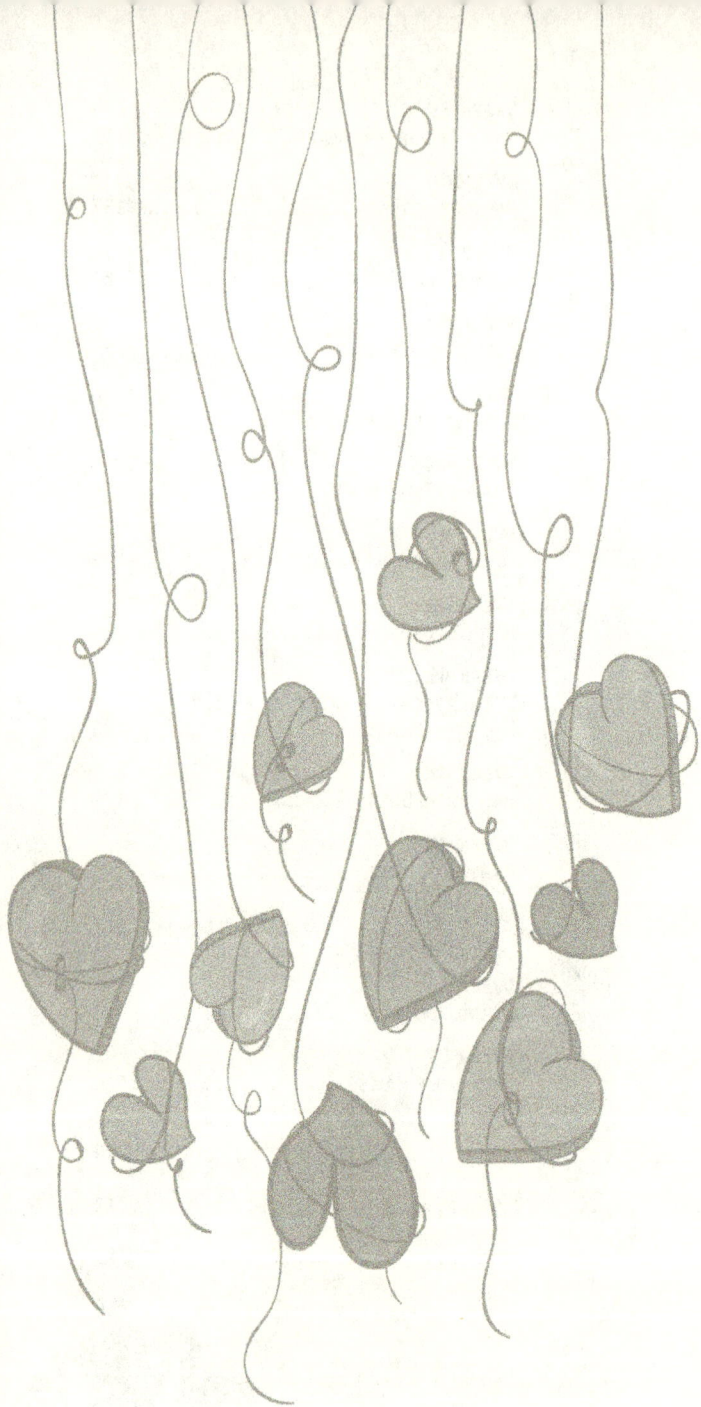

INTRODUCTION

WELCOME TO 52 LOVE. NO, IT'S NOT AN UNBALANCED TENNIS SCORE. IT'S
52 weeks of intimacy tips for you to try with your partner. In our fast-paced lives, it's more important than ever to preserve relationships with the people occupying our hearts. And unlike tennis, with *52 Love*, all parties who play the game win.

One year, inspired by the romantic tango between the characters in the novel I was writing, I used my website to share weekly suggestions on how to increase intimacy. After the blog's success, I hosted *The 52 Love Podcast*, which led to this book:

52 Love: Weekly Love Lessons in Bite-Sized Bits

52 Love shares suggestions in easy-to-follow vignettes. Using similar teachings to Gary Chapman's *The 5 Love Languages* and Stephen Covey's *The 7 Habits of Highly Effective Marriage*, *52 Love* delivers weekly tips through a modern lens. Embracing **Love is Love** culture, these lessons improve intimacy for couples of any gender, age, sexual orientation, or identity.

The suggestions in this book work interchangeably with men, women, or non-binary people, regardless of how they couple. To avoid repeated use of *her/his, his or her, they,* or a lengthy list of *xem, hir, em, per,* and *ver,* each tip sticks with a single he/she gender, alternating between weeks. My hope is that when reading through the series, you'll be comfortable inserting your preferred pronouns.

Whether you are new to one another or have cherished each other for years, *52 Love* aims to revive waning passions or fuel fires that still burn. Though most of the tips are inspired from personal experience, research, or ways my fictional characters wooed one another, *52 Love* focuses less on my journey and more on you, the reader.

Thank you very much for trusting me to guide you on this year-long excursion. After each lesson, look for **Love Bites**—additional morsels to nibble on after the week's main course. By the end of this series, these tips, discussion prompts, and exercises should show you how to expand your palette, enhance your relationship, and ultimately **use Love as a Verb**.

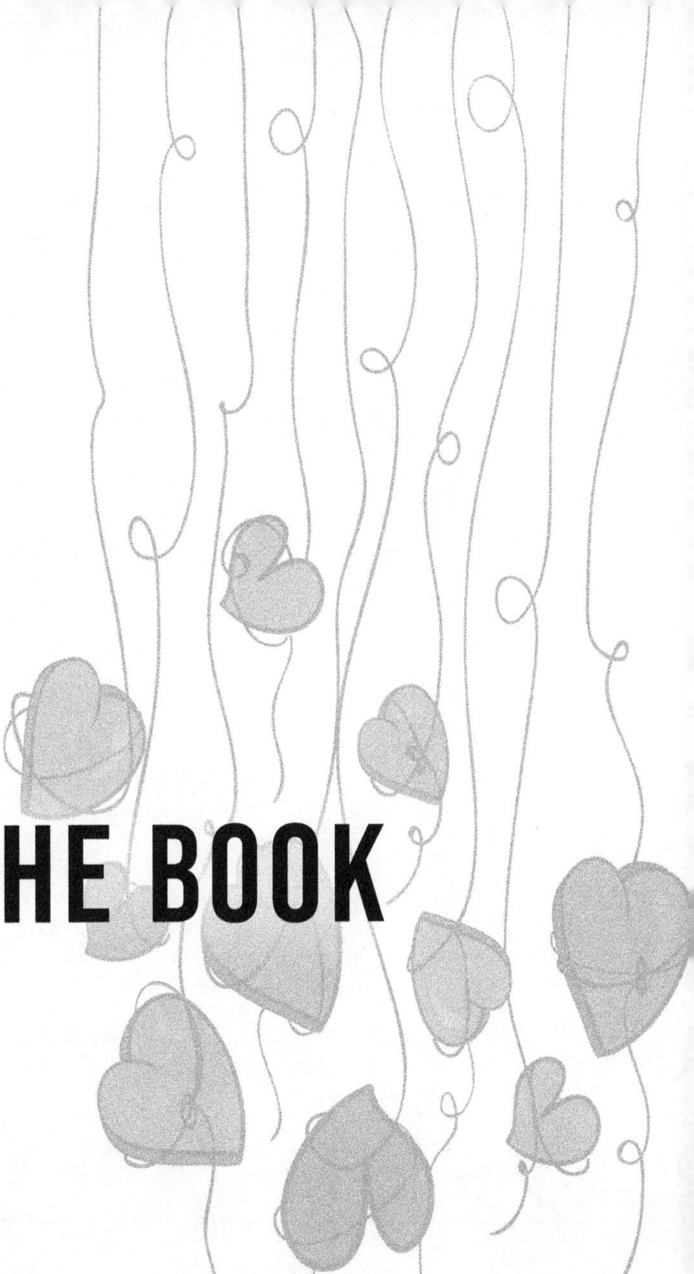

THE BOOK

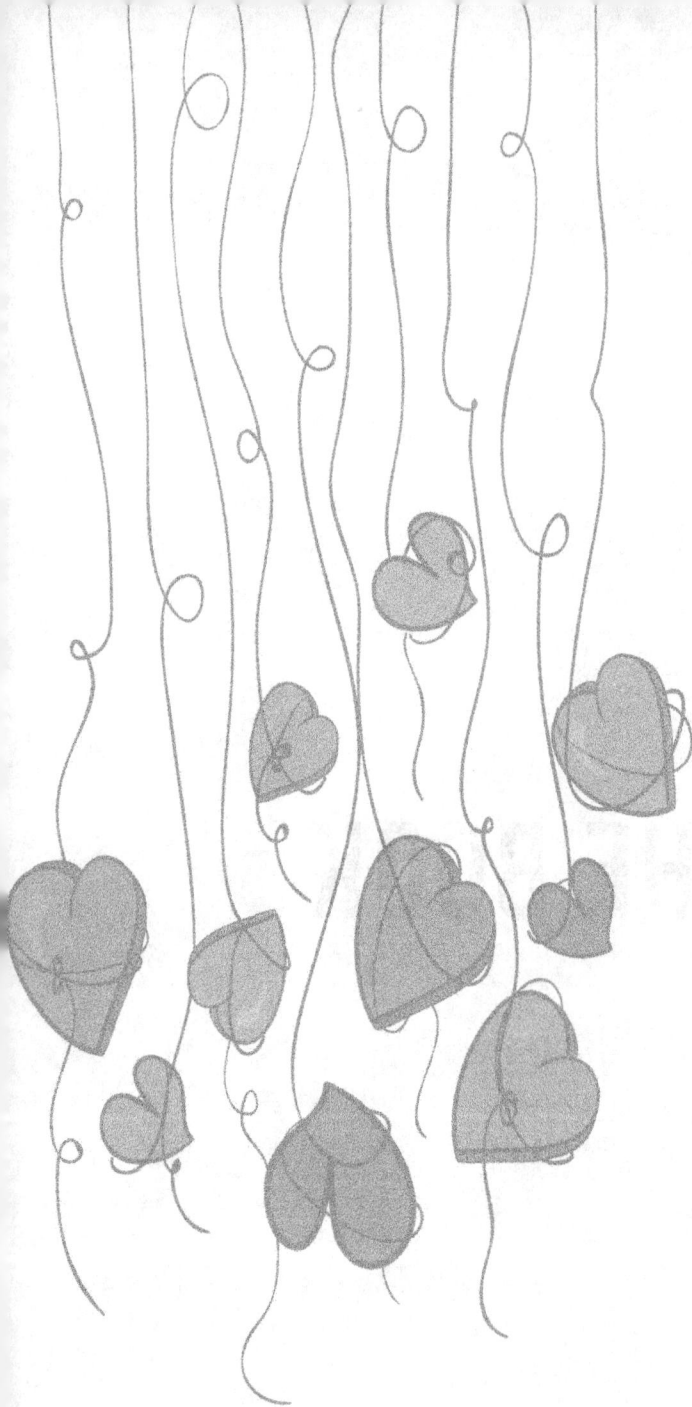

WEEK 1

Tea Time

COLD WEATHER PRESIDES OVER MOST OF THE COUNTRY RIGHT NOW. CHILLY air penetrates the walls and seeps into our bones. What better season to heat things up with your partner? The next time she comes in after an outdoor jog or a day of gardening, bring water to a gentle boil and brew her favorite tea. Prepare her usual accompaniments: cream, sugar, honey, and of course, a dainty spoon.

If she's not a tea drinker (is that possible?), heat a cup of milk for hot chocolate. Yes, *milk*, not water. This represents your affection, after all. Some prefer this with marshmallows melting on the surface or cinnamon sprinkled on top. In my experience, whipped cream—and plenty of it—works best. The higher the swirl, the more love you convey. Make it pretty. Aesthetics always count.

This concept works equally well with coffee, spiced cider, or (Yum!) a hot toddy. Whatever your partner prefers will taste that much better when made with love.

Leave the kitchen as clean as you found it. While she cradles her cold hands over a steaming cup, relishing her new toasty glow, tidy the mess. Clear all evidence. Clean out the tea infuser or toss the used bag. Rinse the whipped cream nozzle before returning it to the refrigerator. Wipe debris from the counter. Rather than negate your generous act by piling more work on your partner, let clearing the aftermath serve as your final loving touch.

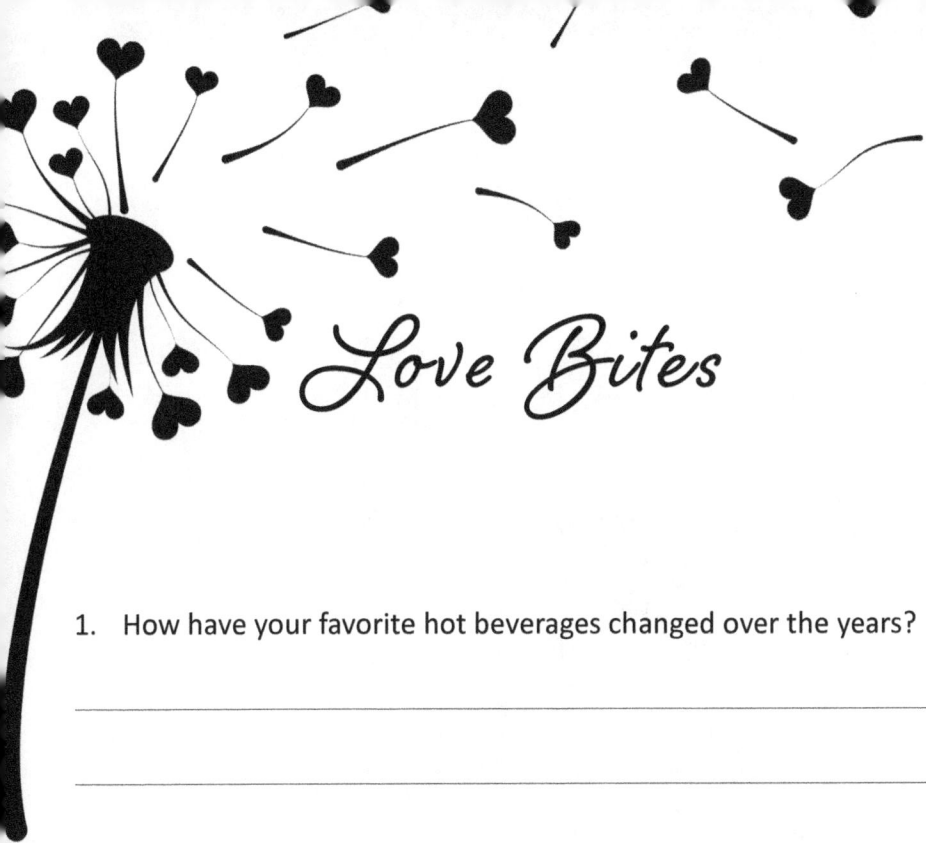

Love Bites

1. How have your favorite hot beverages changed over the years?

_____

_____

_____

2. When did you first try your favorite hot beverages? What were the circumstances?

_____

_____

_____

3. What other memories do your favorites evoke?

_____

_____

_____

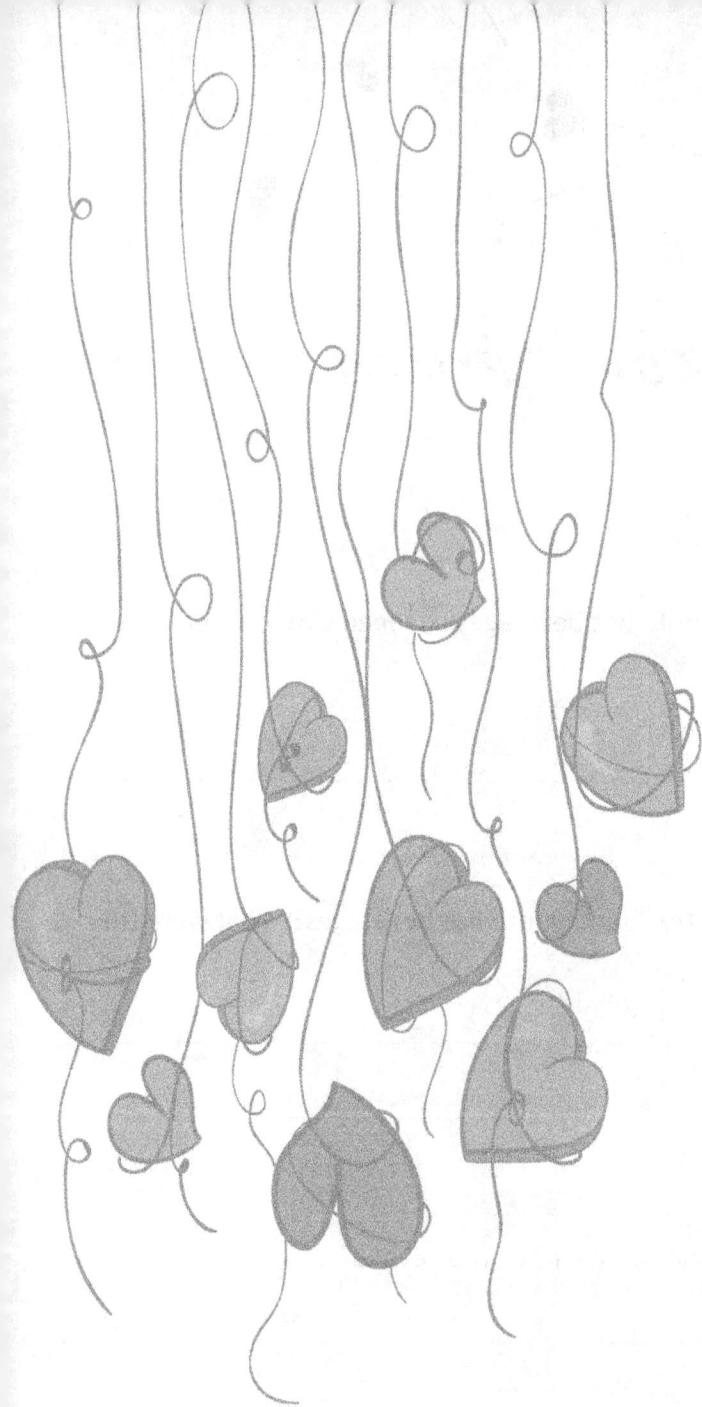

WEEK 2

All Ears

COMMUNICATION IS ESSENTIAL TO A HEALTHY RELATIONSHIP. ONE OF THE best ways couples can show love is by asking about each other's day and (here's the most important part) listening to the answer.

Remember the days before you were partners, when you two would spend hours chatting? When the rest of the world fell away and time belonged only to you? So often, the hustle and bustle of life hinders these quality conversations. Texting can't replace the intimacy of one-on-one dialogue between lovers. Important emotional clues are communicated through voice and facial expression. This week, gift your full, in-person attention when your partner shares details from his day.

Block distractions, stay focused, and ask thoughtful questions along the way. This isn't about pulling information from him. It's not an interrogation. In fact, you should do very little of the talking. Avoid steering the conversation toward subject matter that interests you. *He* interests you. That's why you're listening.

Even if he sticks to topics that don't appeal to you, hear his trivialities with the same interest you would if he'd been away on a long trip and came home to share the experience with you. Shut down your phone, switch off the television, sit on the edge of your chair, and truly focus on him. Letting him feel like he captivates you will spark an energy exchange that benefits you both. You may just find his story ends with an unexpected twist. And even if it doesn't, he'll hear the point of *your* story: he is loved by you.

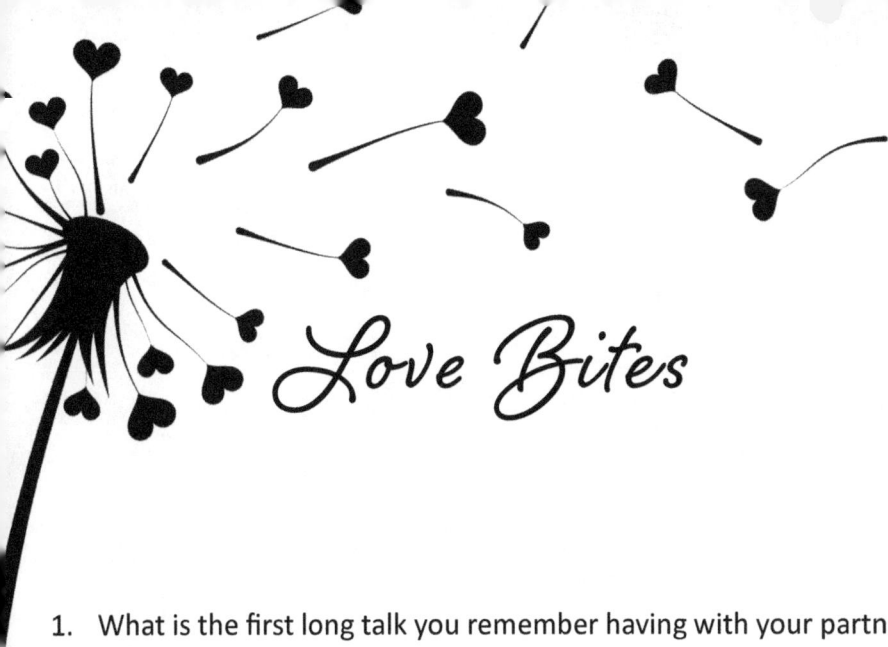

Love Bites

1. What is the first long talk you remember having with your partner?

_____

_____

_____

2. Share an example of a time your partner communicated a deep interest in you.

_____

_____

_____

3. For each of you, which body cues best communicate attention?

_____

_____

_____

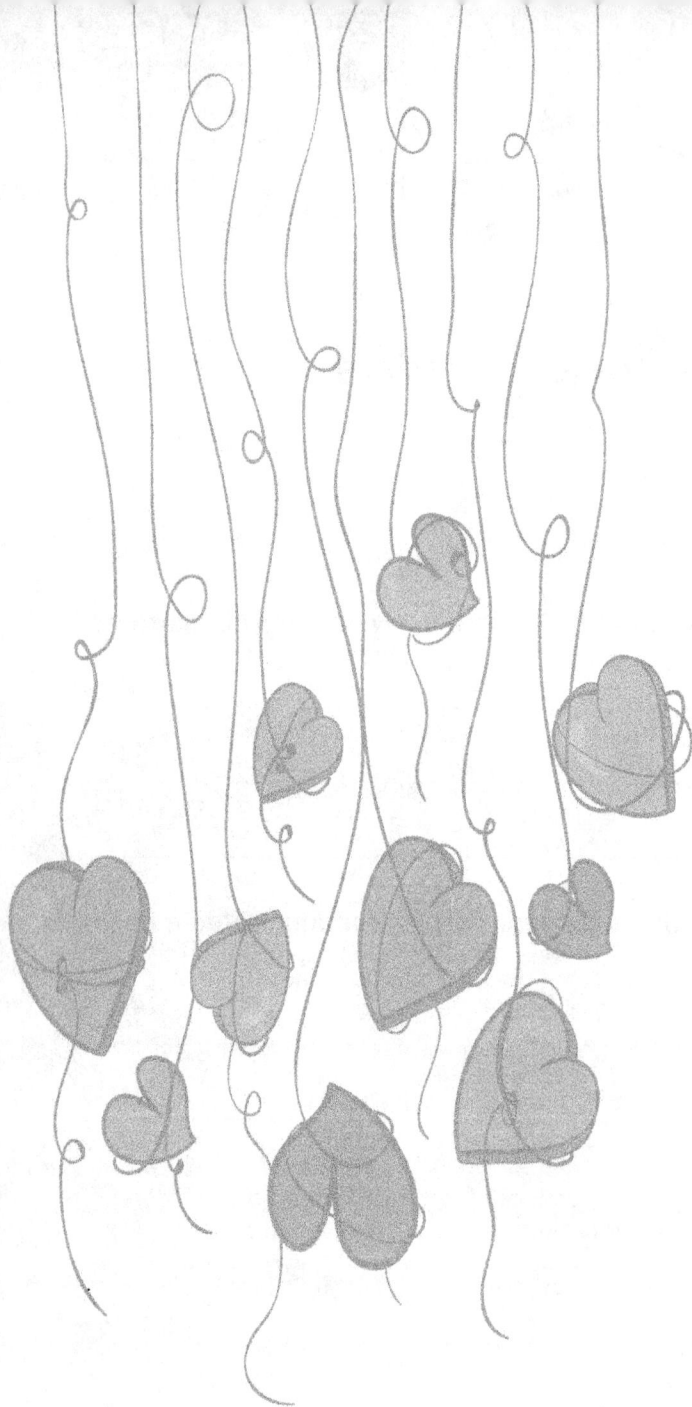

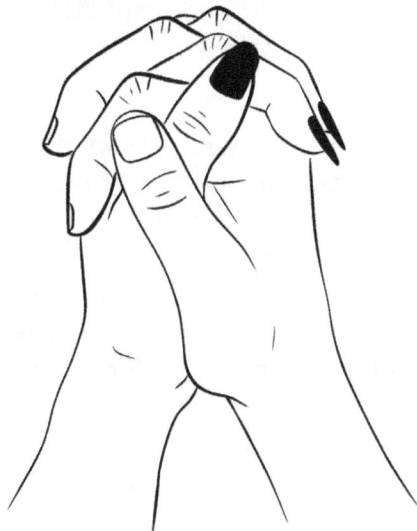

WEEK 3

The Whole World

I'M ALWAYS TOUCHED WHEN I SEE AN ELDERLY COUPLE WALKING HAND-in-hand. Relationships evolve over time. No matter what stage you and your partner have reached, hold hands through this leg of your journey. It may seem like a small expression, but sometimes the smallest gestures wield the greatest power.

In any type of relationship, hand-holding expresses a shared connection. With your partner, holding hands cements a link, binds you together, locks you as one. And no matter the size difference, holding hands demonstrates that you fit together. This simple act communicates complex signals—signals that delve beneath the skin's surface to root their message deep within your partner. Interlock fingers to express a desired attachment. Hold tight to convey solidarity. Stroke your thumb across bare skin as your promise of pleasures to come.

There's a reason Shakespeare said, "Let lips do what hands do." That sensual skin-on-skin contact mirrors the press of two lips. Much like kissing, hand-holding produces oxytocin, which in turn stimulates dopamine and serotonin. Hands and fingers possess the most nerve endings in the body. Imagine the potency in each subtle skin-brushed sweep.

Hand-holding makes a proud public statement that declares: "I'm with her!" It offers a comforting voice that murmurs: "I'm with you." Above all, hand-holding shares an intimacy that whispers: "*I love you.*"

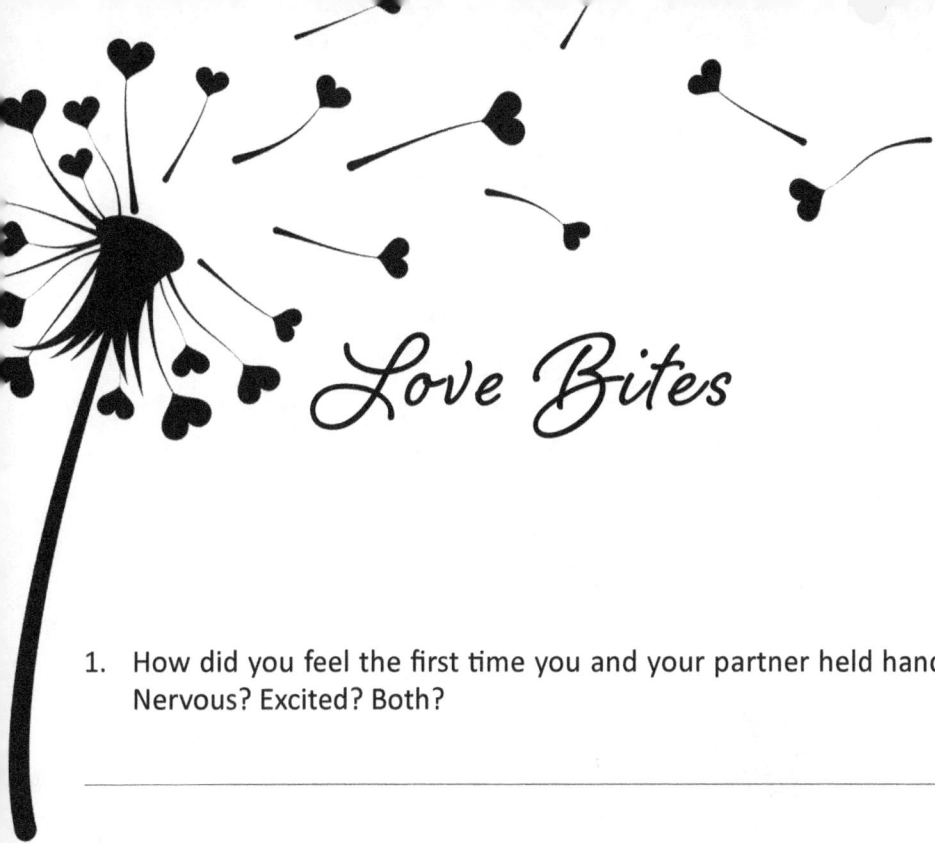

Love Bites

1. How did you feel the first time you and your partner held hands? Nervous? Excited? Both?

_____

_____

_____

2. When you hold hands, how long does it take for the transfer of heat to spread evenly between you? Can you follow the path?

_____

_____

_____

3. How long can the two of you hold hands without talking?

_____

_____

_____

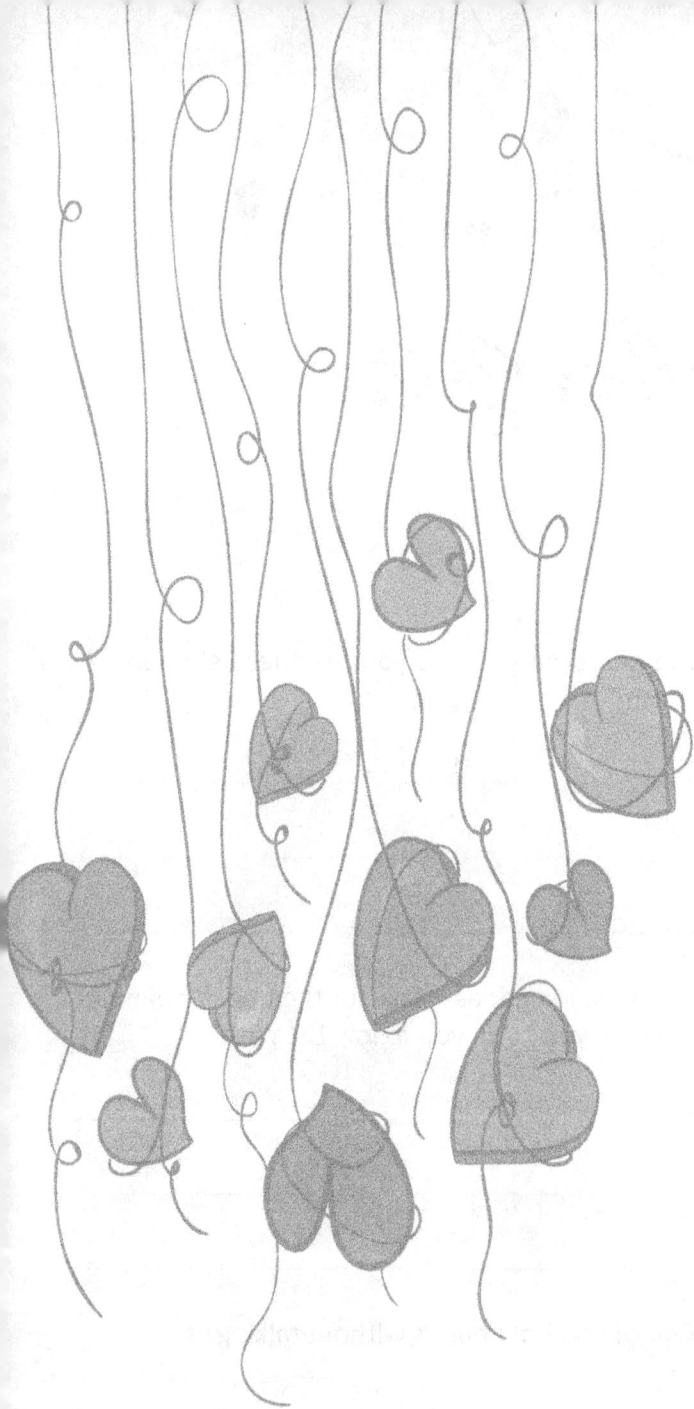

WEEK 4

Step by Step

NEVER UNDERESTIMATE THE VALUE OF AGENDA-FREE TIME. ODDLY ENOUGH, one of the best ways I've found to block the outside world is to go … outside. The next time you want to showcase your affection, grab your partner for a healthy jaunt outdoors.

Let this alone time remind that you need only each other. Fresh air and exercise work wonders for the soul. Walking alone increases blood flow, reduces stress, and promotes a healthy mind and body. With a partner, it produces much more. A relaxing stroll can help you both decompress from the fast-paced hustle of your all-too-busy lives. Clear your minds from the daily burdens and simply enjoy one another's company. Leave phones at home. Forgo overstimulating technology. Instead, embrace each other.

Make memories by enjoying the journey. Ignore your destination and your step count; your goal is together time. While outdoors, share the visuals that often go unnoticed: plants in bloom, critters at play, impressive cloud formations. Turn to your partner and absorb the way the sun highlights the sparkle in his eyes.

This focused attention strengthens your bond. Prioritizing time together shows him how much he means to you when you're apart. Little efforts like this accumulate over time and build the foundation for a lifetime of love.

As a bonus, use this opportunity to incorporate the *52 Love* lessons from the last three weeks. Hold hands during your stroll, listen with intent, and treat your sweetie to a hot beverage after you come in from the cold. Who knows? After your walk, you may catch a second wind, which could lead to other intimate endeavors. You'll certainly sleep better afterward.

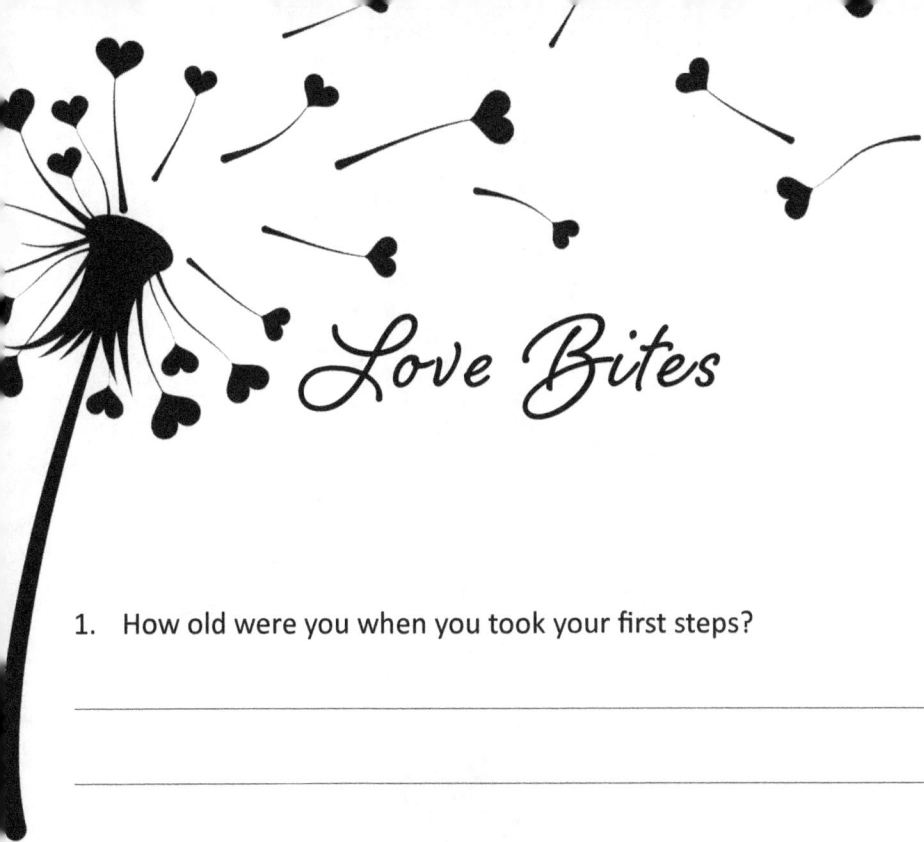

Love Bites

1. How old were you when you took your first steps?

   _____

   _____

   _____

2. What are your favorite visuals when walking outside? Foliage? Fauna? Cloud formations? The moon?

   _____

   _____

   _____

3. Would you rather walk barefoot over a hot, sandy beach or frolic through a field of flowers? Why?

   _____

   _____

   _____

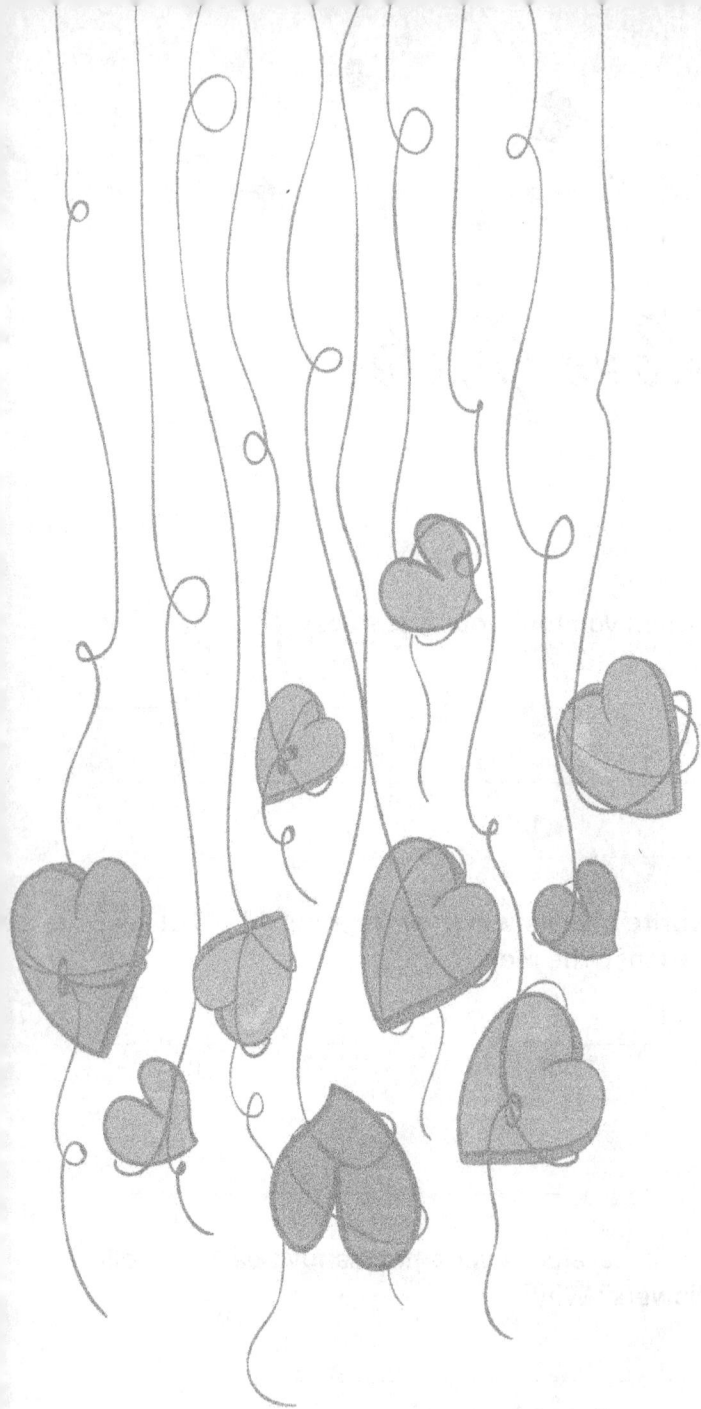

WEEK 5

Fervent Verses

YOU DON'T HAVE TO BE EDWARD BULWER-LYTTON TO RECOGNIZE THE power of the pen. Nor must you be Shakespeare to power your pen effectively. This week, celebrate your powerful passion by penning your love in a poem.

Poetry reaches the soul. Whispered words. Perfumed prose. Kisses caressing your core. A poem crafted from love can penetrate to the root of what makes her yours.

Poetry consists of symbols that communicate strong emotion or beauty. As a means to express love, a handwritten poem lasts as a permanent reminder of your affection. This gesture will express your sentiment on multiple levels. Regardless of your partner's love language or your skills as a wordsmith, she will appreciate the time you spent composing, the prose that confesses your heart, and the physical gift that captures it all.

Experiment with your poem. Let your creative juices flow. Try a dirty limerick, craft an acrostic list with adjectives that describe her, or pen an ode to her lips. The tone can range from the tenderness of "How Do I Love Thee?" to the titillation of "May I Feel?" No need to study poetic format to script your loving words. The beauty of poetic license means you need not limit your possibilities. Whether free prose, haiku, limerick, or sonnet, the important thing is to capture your heart on the page.

Love Bites

1. What is your favorite type of poem? Free verse, rhyming, haiku? Why?

_____

_____

_____

2. Share your favorite poem. What is it you appreciate about it?

_____

_____

_____

3. Music is poetry. What song lyrics remind you of your partner?

_____

_____

_____

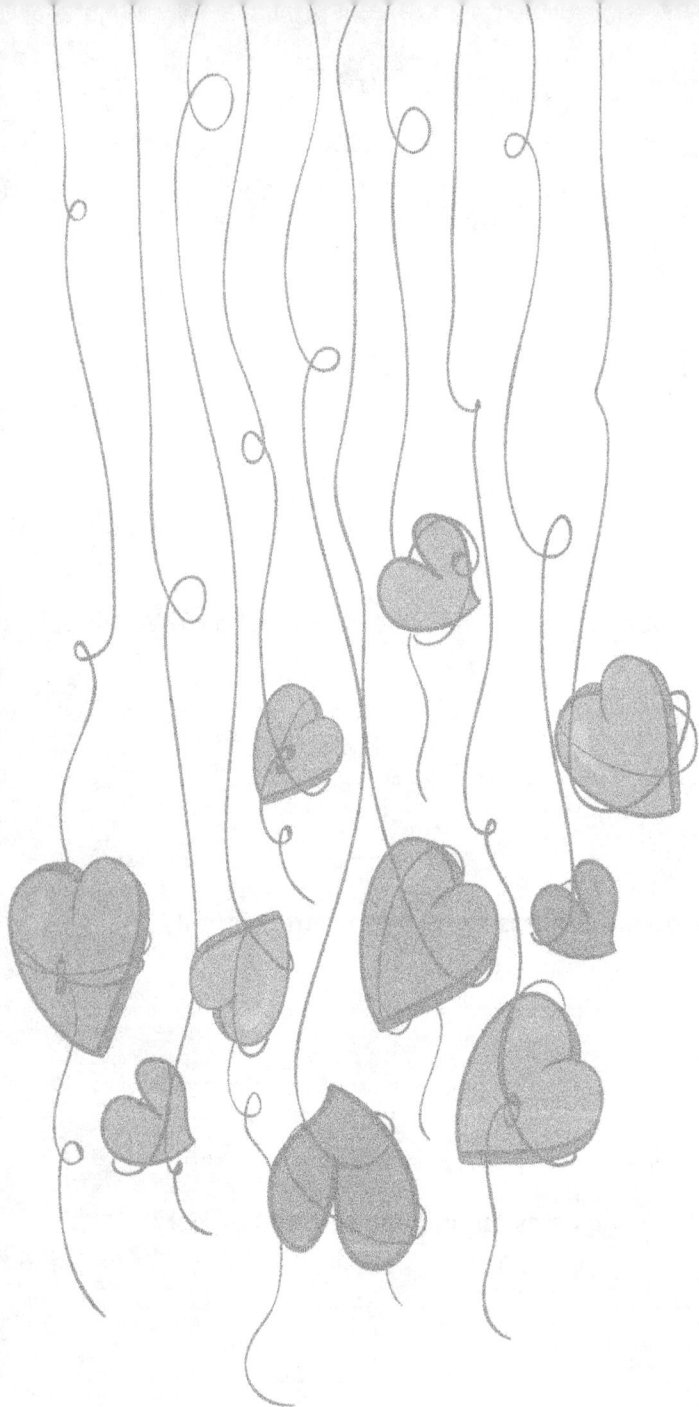

WEEK 6

Playtime

FLOWERS AND CHOCOLATES PERFUME THE AIR; WE'RE CLOSE TO Valentine's Day. Those tried-and-true gifts are great—thoughtful even—51 weeks out of the year, but on this special day, get creative. Galvanize your love life with a sexy game.

While there are dozens of premade options you can (and should!) buy, this week's tip focuses on games you can play without the added expense.

Your game can be as simple as strip poker, or better yet, strip Twister. Straightforward carefree fun. If you want to tantalize your lover's brain as well as his body, try adding a strip-tease to games like Scrabble or Scattergories which require some measure of thinking. I guarantee concentration will become more challenging with each item tossed to the floor.

Run out of clothes? For a bonus side-game, number your six favorite body parts, then roll a die to determine which one you kiss. Play like this until you can no longer keep your hands (or your lips) off each other.

More adventurous lovers can give role-play a try. You and your partner choose a scenario and improvise as you progress. Not quite comfortable with that level? Start with a game of fantasy charades, but instead of performing solo, act them out on one another.

If you're somewhere in between, replace the list of actions with a box of costumes. Whichever item you draw from the box inspires the scene you perform on each other. For every cheerleader, French maid, and sexy nurse fantasy you bring to life, your partner can portray your firefighter, naughty cop, and randy repairman. (Full disclosure: I stole those last two from one of my manuscripts.)

The best part about these sexy games is that even for the most competitive players, no matter the outcome, you both win. And if you truly need the title, schedule a rematch to sate all your cravings.

Love Bites

1. Name three games that would be improved by nudity.

_____

_____

_____

2. How competitive are the two of you?

_____

_____

_____

3. For these games, would you rather lose and be ravished or win and do the ravishing?

_____

_____

_____

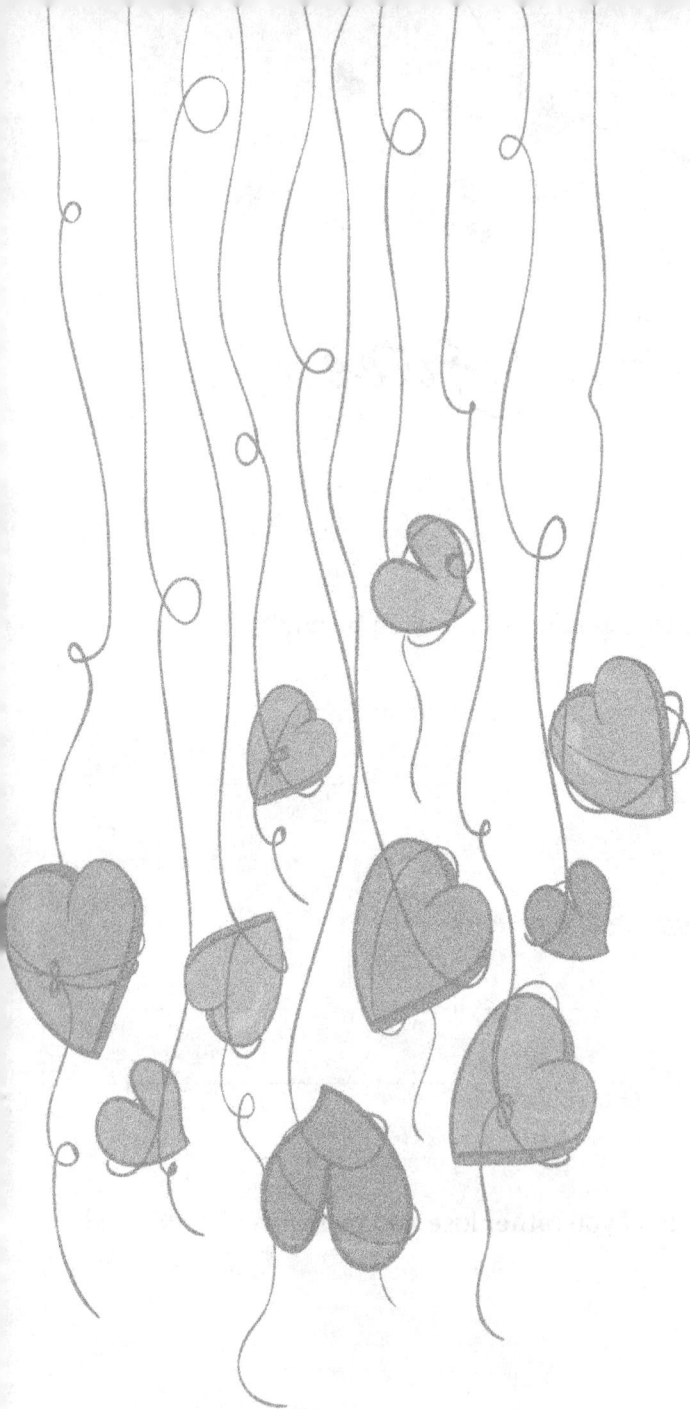

WEEK 7

Tango for Two

PARTNERS WHO SWEAT TOGETHER, STAY TOGETHER. IT'S TRUE. FOR THIS week's tip, I'm stealing from my character Lucian's arsenal. His recommendation: stay in for an evening of dancing.

That's right, dance at home, where there's no cover charge or waiting in line. No need to wear uncomfortable shoes. Better still, you control the music. No overplayed pop anthems to spoil the mood. Your playlist will set the tone for the evening be it "At Last," "Let's Get it On," or simply "Dancing Machine."

Whether literally or figuratively, dancing benefits the heart. Burning calories together elevates endorphins and raises your pulse. Cardio boost aside, the time spent close to your partner reconnects your bodies. Heavy breaths, tangled limbs, hips moving in sync. Your bodies work together toward a shared goal: mutual passion.

Dancing will help increase your bond. Shortness of breath and a racing pulse mirror the sensations of falling in love. Revive emotional memories as you sway together. Glide fingers over warm skin to rest your hand in the swoop of your partner's back. Press chest to chest. Inspire desire with a light sweep of your fingers and the firm grip of your gaze. Wrapped in this much sensuality, you can't help but arouse renewed affection.

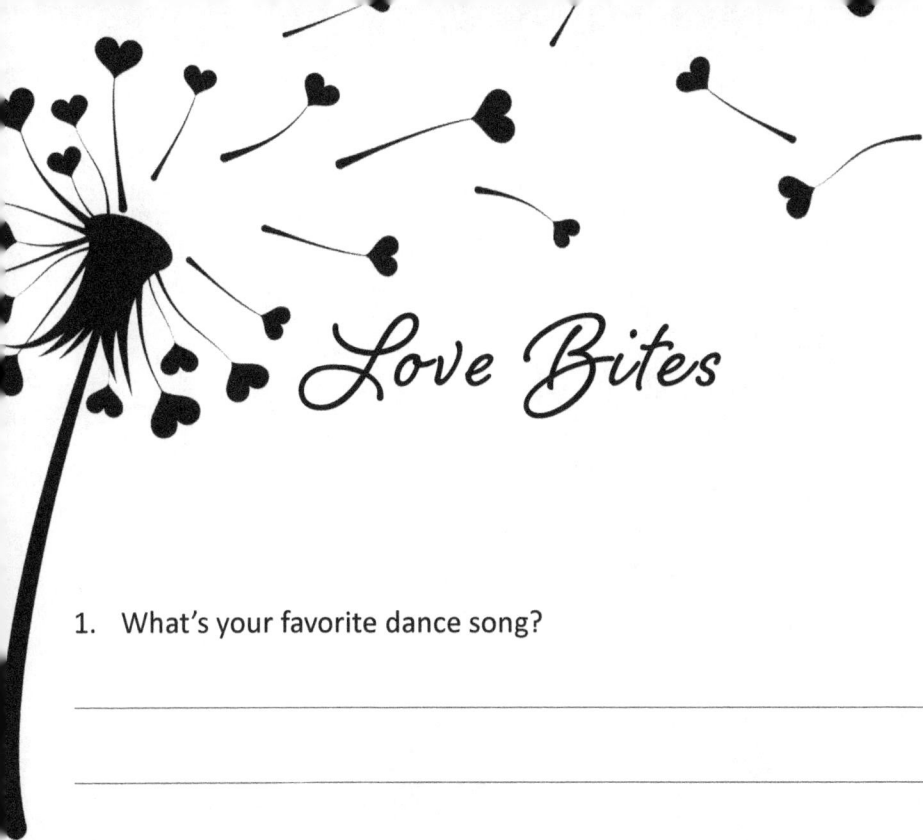

Love Bites

1. What's your favorite dance song?

_____

_____

_____

2. Do you prefer quick paced songs or slow jams when dancing with your partner?

_____

_____

_____

3. Discuss which ten songs would make up the perfect playlist for dancing with each other. (Bonus points for creating this playlist!)

_____

_____

_____

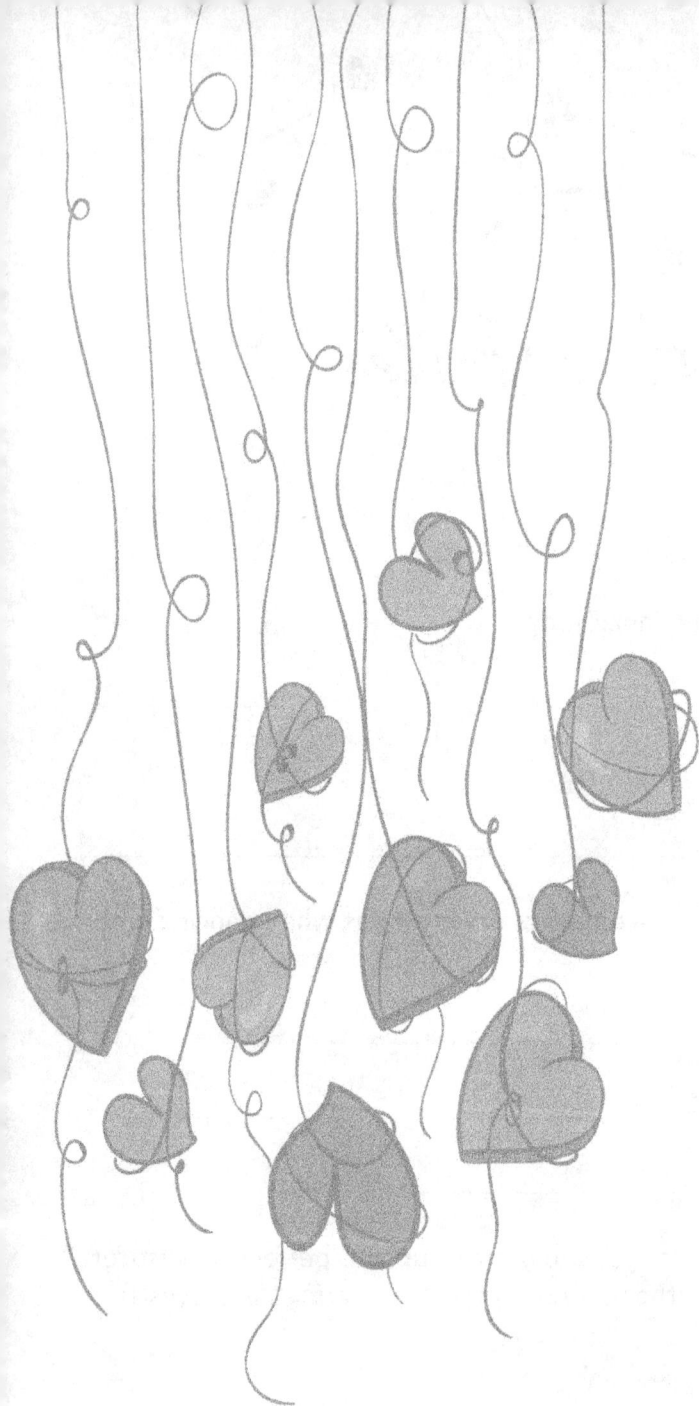

WEEK 8

Get Toasty

LIVING IN VEGAS, I'M NEVER IN A RUSH FOR OUR SCORCHING SUMMERS.
Yet sometimes, the winters can feel just as harsh. Years ago, one fierce
February flurry brought with it a temperature drop that prompted this
52 Love suggestion: counter the cold by creating your own heat.

Bake dessert for your partner. There is nothing more delicious than
fresh-baked chocolate chip cookies straight out of the oven, their gooey
rich flavors melting over your tongue. Involved with a pie guy? A warm
apple pastry should heat his heart. Even if you don't bake his treat from
scratch, the loving gesture will fire his affection.

Heat a towel for your honey. While he washes off the cold day, toss
a towel in the dryer, then bring it to him when he's done. No dryer?
No problem. Have him shower while your cookies bake. After the next
batch, turn off the oven, place the towel on a clean baking sheet, and
set it in the still-hot oven for 2-3 minutes. Resume baking while he dries.

Cocoon yourselves in a plush blanket. Wrap the corners around your bodies and snuggle within its warm folds. Kindle this intimate moment with subtle heated brushes along the arms or thighs. You're only limited by where your hands can reach.

Separately, each of these tips creates heat. Combined, they ignite a hot storm of sweet sentiment that strengthens your existing bond. Bake those cookies, warm that towel, snuggle together, then enjoy each other in the throes of burning passion. Summer will be here before we know it. Take advantage of these cooler days, and let the chill do what it will.

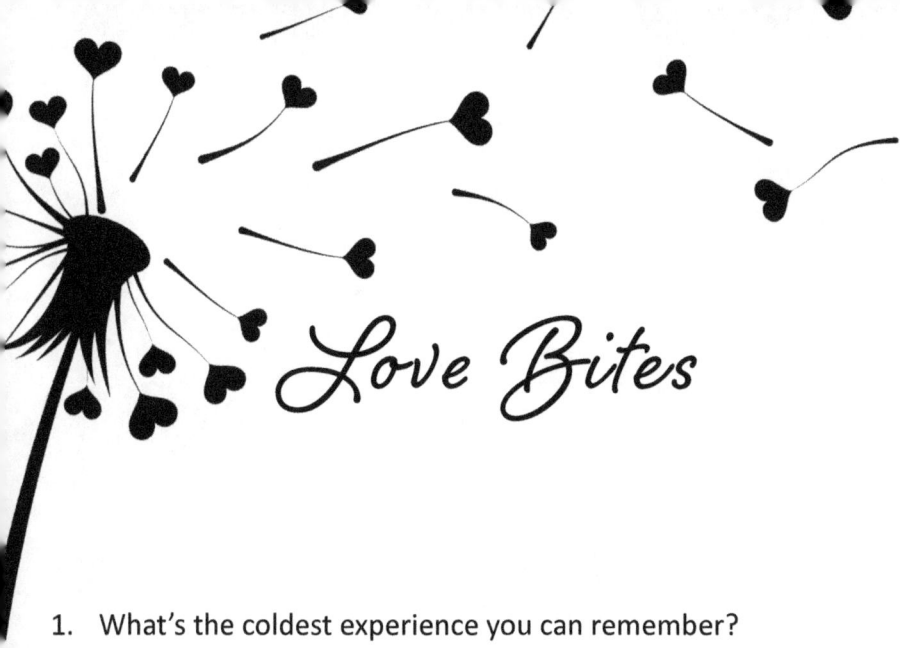

Love Bites

1. What's the coldest experience you can remember?

_____

_____

_____

2. Do you prefer cold weather or hot weather? Why?

_____

_____

_____

3. Which desserts taste better warm?

_____

_____

_____

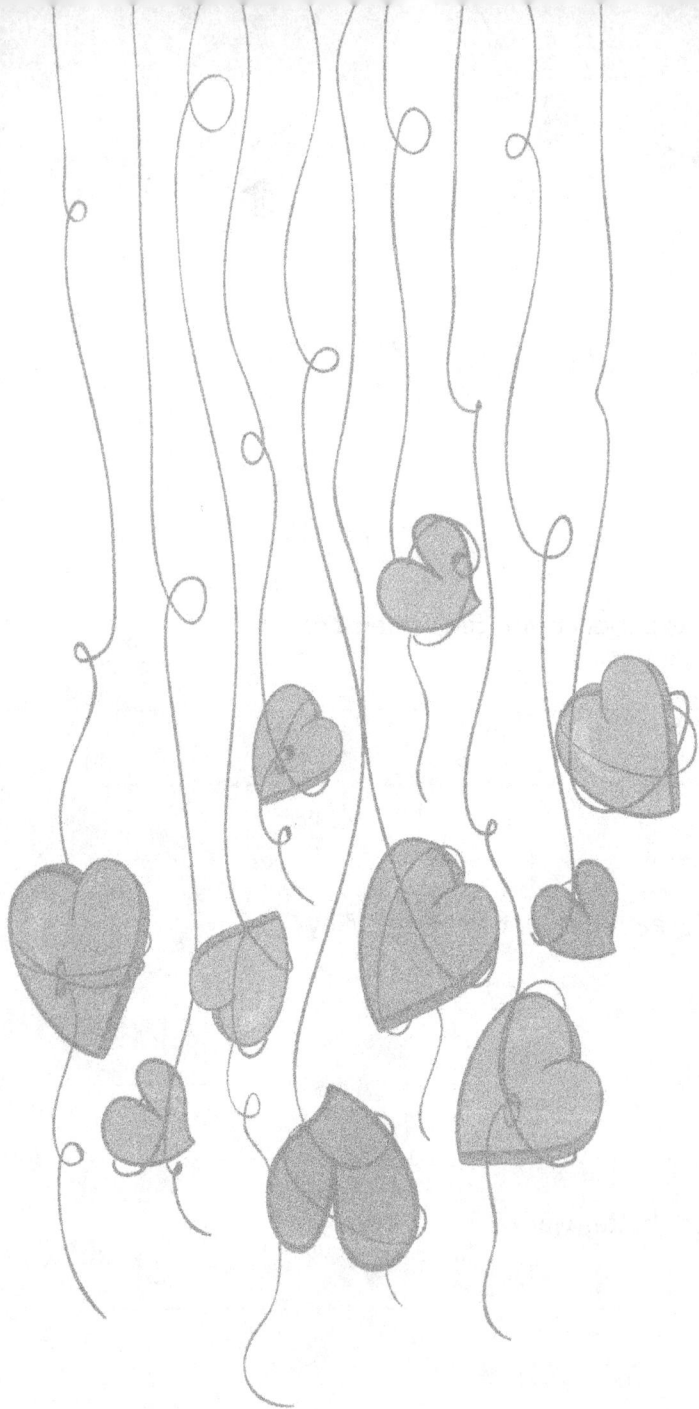

WEEK 9

Talk Dirty to Me

LANGUAGE IS A SENSUAL TOOL. FOR ME, FEW THINGS AROUSE LIKE A large vocabulary. Yet even the most educated indulge in naughty wordplay. The lead character in my first manuscript (Sasha) insists on always speaking with the grace of a lady. Determined to change that, her devilish beau threatens that, once permitted to ravish her, she should prepare herself for the passion he'll unleash on her "and the league of obscenities that follow." Now, there's a man who understands the value in your next *52 Love* lesson: titillating with your tongue.

Sapiosexual or not, a great way to show love is to make your partner feel desired. Public dirty talk does more than *show* love; it improves your sex life. By public, I don't mean for you to broadcast your intimacy. Rather, in between mingling at your next social gathering, lean in close and whisper your sweet somethings within the public setting. Repeated throughout the evening, your covert acts will provide the thrill of getting away with something right under people's noses and stimulate your partner on a deeper level.

Whispering feels important. Not only are you putting your mouth close to your partner's ear, you're speaking words for her alone. The soft tickle of your breath travels through every nerve and tingles body parts to attention.

Not sure what to say? When in doubt, stick with the basics. Tell her what you like about what she's done in the past and how you plan to pleasure her in the future. What do you want to do to her? Where and how do you want to do it?

If you're new to dirty talk, try these starter phrases. As you pass by your partner from one mini crowd to the next, take her aside and say, "The way you look in that dress has me crazy," or "I can't get enough of you. When we get home, I'm going to____!"

Feeling more confident? Let her know how her appearance is affecting your body or that you love the way she tastes. Lick the tip of her ear to remind her how your tongue feels. Tell her how you'd like to slam her against the wall and take her in front of all those people. Threaten to have your way with her right there at your event. "What if I just bent you over the counter right now?"

Make it clear that you can't stop thinking about her. Catch her eye from across the room, raise one brow, and pretend to say your next temptation. To avoid getting caught by champion lip readers, mouth your phone number or some other innocent tidbit. The important thing is that even from a distance, you're fueling future fires.

By the end of the night, make promises no mortal could deliver. "I'm going to make you scream enough to scare the neighbors." Even if you don't follow through, these frequent teases are enough to have her drag you into the bedroom the second you get home and inspire the delectable details in your next round of public dirty talk.

Love Bites

1. How does it make you feel when your partner vocalizes sexual intentions?

_____

_____

_____

2. How comfortable are you with voicing similar intentions?

_____

_____

_____

3. What type of feedback do you enjoy during lovemaking?

_____

_____

_____

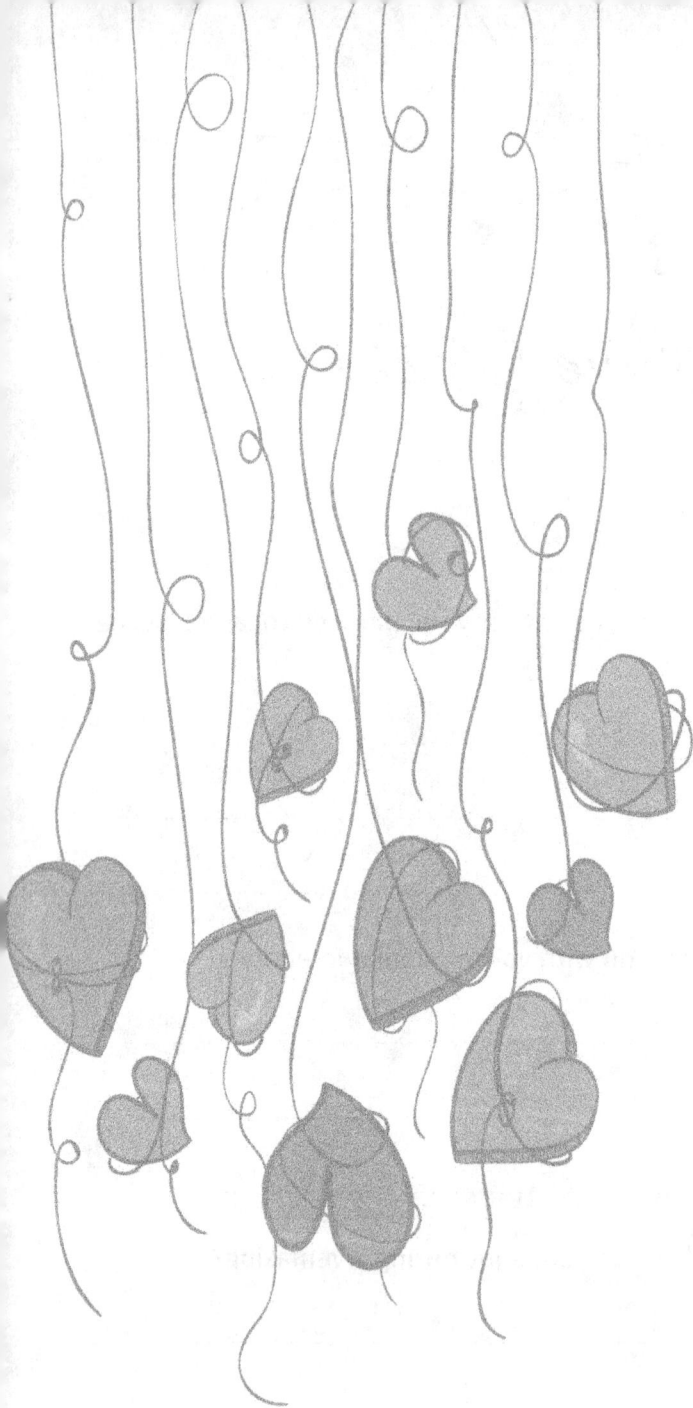

WEEK 10

One for the Books

FOR WEEK 10 OF 52 LOVE, BUY YOUR PARTNER A BOOK. THIS IS NOT THE time to gift that book you think he *needs* to read. You want him to feel appreciated, not judged. Try a selection from his favorite author or comic book series. If he owns the whole collection, buy a book *about* that author or those beloved characters. No favorite scribe? Try a graphic novel or book on a topic he likes. Make it clear that you have thought about his interests and searched for something that would suit him.

Take it one step further and read the book in tandem so he has a discussion partner. This tells him that you are aware of his tastes, and those tastes are important to you. Translation: *he* is important to you.

As with any gift, proper presentation morphs it from mundane to memorable. It's easy to say it's the thought that counts, but fancy packaging represents the extent of that thought. Whether you arrange it with tissue paper in a gift bag or dress it with decorative wrap, your personal touch provides a special boost that speaks the volumes between, "I found this while out shopping for myself" versus "I chose to buy this because I love you."

Maximize his pleasure by including a custom bookmark. One of life's small annoyances is trying to find something to mark your place when you start a new book. Consider purchasing the book and accessories at a local indie bookstore instead of online. With no email announcing the gift's arrival, he won't see it coming. Your in-person purchase is more personal and highlights the extra effort you made.

Best of all, books can be enjoyed again and again. The contents last a lifetime, as does the memory of receiving the gift. And every time he sees the book, reads it, recalls the story, or uses your customized book-mark, he'll associate it with the fond memory of your gesture.

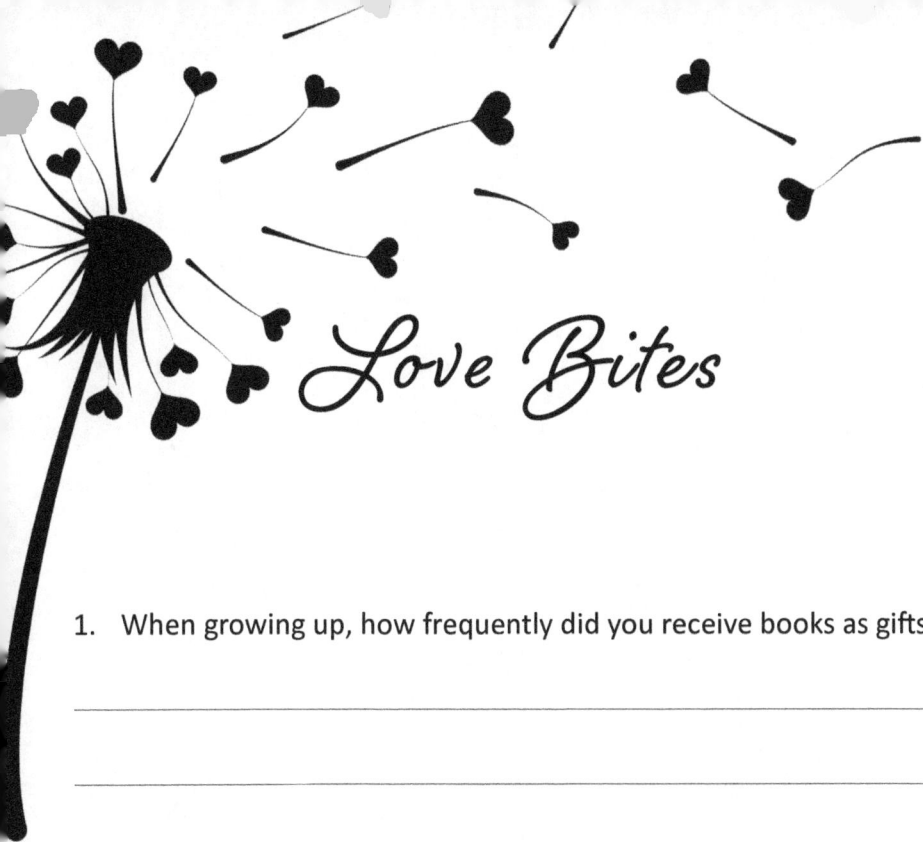

Love Bites

1. When growing up, how frequently did you receive books as gifts?

   _____

   _____

   _____

2. What is your favorite type of book?

   _____

   _____

   _____

3. Excluding this week, what's the best book you ever received as a gift?

   _____

   _____

   _____

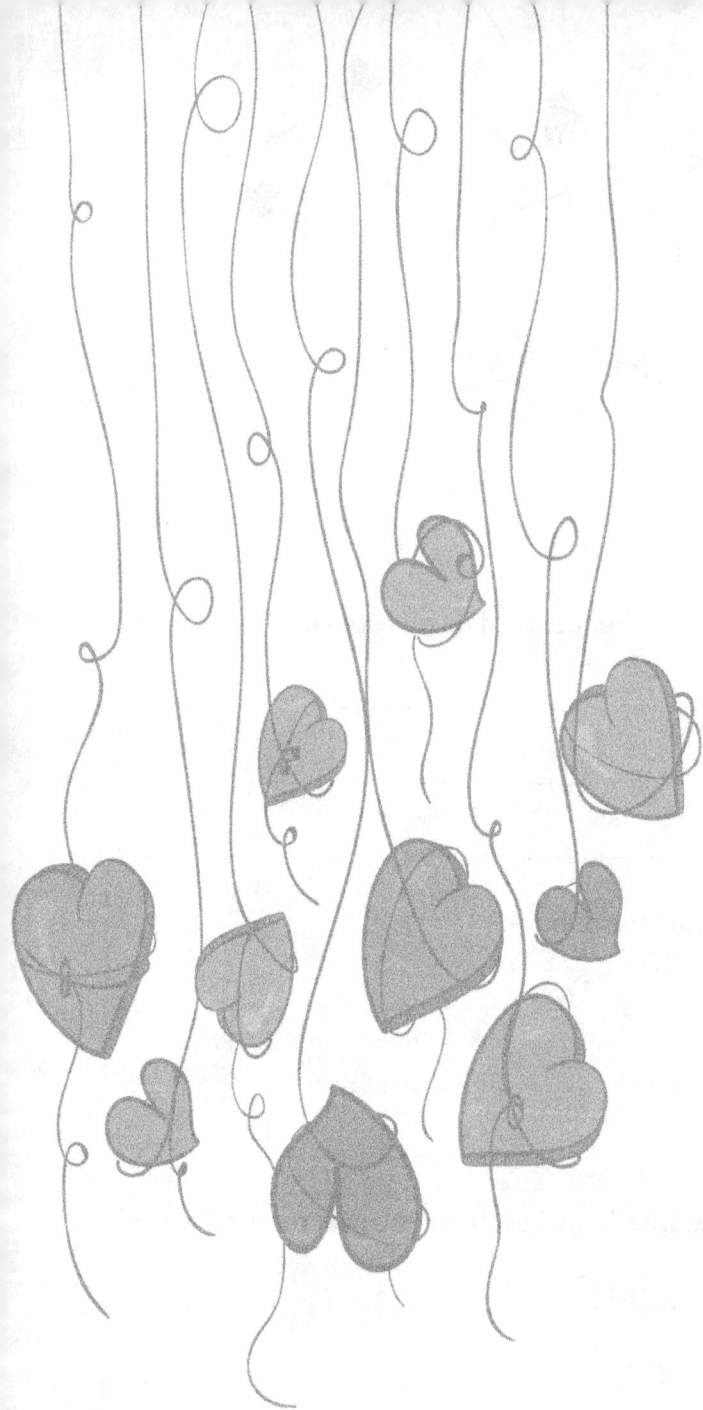

WEEK 11

Count the Little Things

GRATITUDE IS MORE THAN A SOCIAL NICETY; IT'S AN IMPORTANT TOOL that reassures your partner that her efforts are both noticed and appreciated. Most people want to receive thanks for their deeds, even if it's for something that they're supposed to be doing. When life runs smoothly, people often take for granted the small labors that make that possible. For Week 11 of *52 Love*, express your gratitude for those small tasks that improve your life.

Has it been years since you last filled your gas tank or mowed your lawn? Does the laundry fairy fold your socks and place them neatly in your drawer? Do plates and cups magically vanish from the dishwasher and appear in the cupboards? Unless you have a maid or lawn service responsible for those blessings, your partner deserves to hear, "Thank you."

The power in these two words, especially when the recipient isn't expecting them, can make her feel seen, appreciated, and treasured. Saying thank you is a simple and effective way to acknowledge your partner's value to you. Even if you think she knows you appreciate her efforts, strengthen your bond with frequent reminders.

Many people offer these gestures as a reflex to strangers, yet this courtesy is even more important among intimates. Take care to recognize the time your partner spends to make life easier for you, especially given that we are such a time-deprived society. Acknowledge her contributions as a sign of respect. Like the old Tibetan phrase says, "If you take care of the minutes, the years will take care of themselves."

Give your acknowledgment the power it deserves. Don't say it in passing. Make your gratitude a *moment*. Take your partner by the hand, look her in the eyes, and tell her that her efforts matter. Let her know that the things she does make your life more pleasant and enjoyable. And for that, you love her.

Love Bites

1. How often did your parents vocalize gratitude when you were a child?

_____

_____

_____

2. How frequently did you express gratitude to your parents?

_____

_____

_____

3. Name three tasks you appreciate your partner doing.

_____

_____

_____

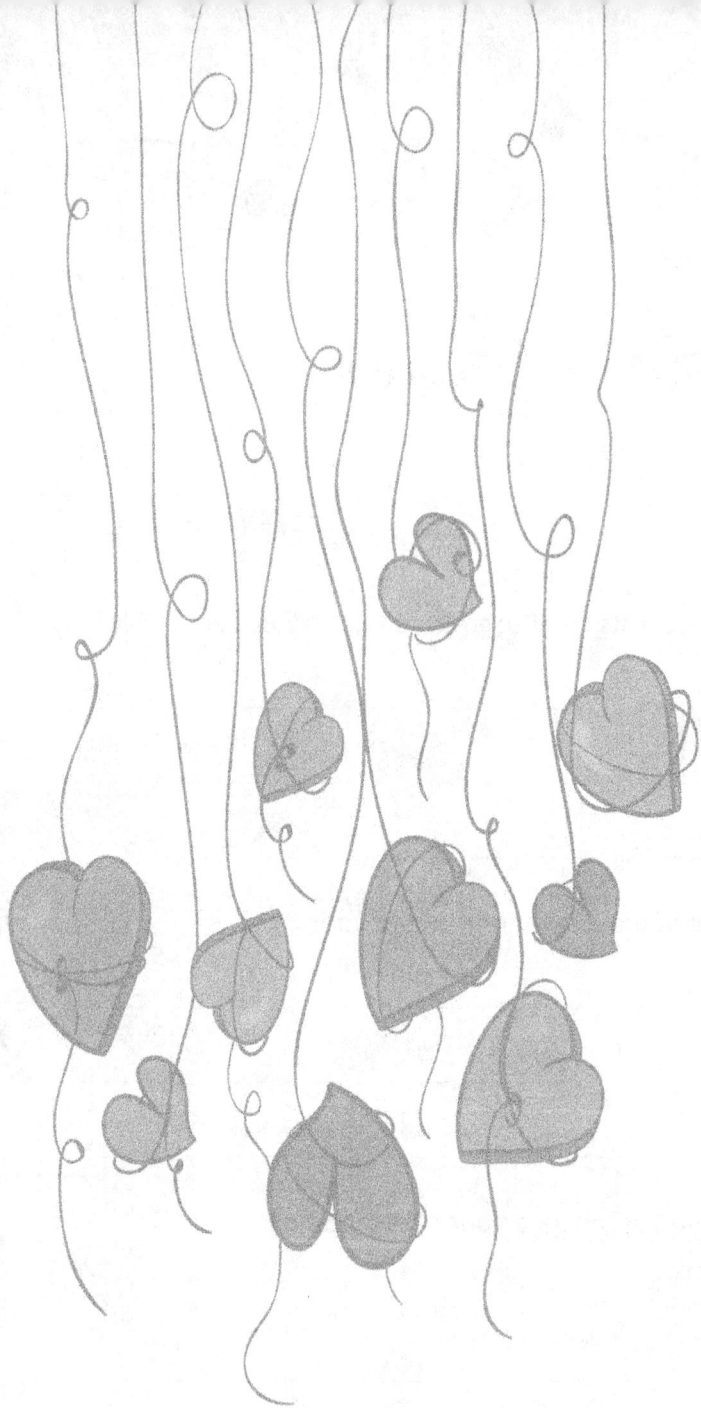

WEEK 12

Close to the Chest

GREETING CARDS SUPPLEMENT HOLIDAY AND BIRTHDAY CELEBRATIONS.
During the in-between days, this unexpected token holds far more weight. The surprise factor alone should brighten your partner's day. More than that, your personal touch will make this a gift to treasure.

Step away from the buzz of social media digital journals and show your partner how you feel with a carefully selected physical symbol of your love. A traditional card lasts longer than the fleeting feel of a text, an email, or even a phone call. Don't weaken your gesture with a flashy, all-too-easy e-card. No videos to view or pixels to peruse. Just a simple, old-fashioned paper reminder of your love.

Allow yourself an afternoon to search the greeting card section of your supermarket or visit a specialty store. Examine the aisles for a card face that suits your partner. Once you narrow your choices to the best covers, read the interior messages until one speaks to you. This gesture is about more than the gift. Humorous or sober. Sexy or sweet. You'll find the time you spent finding the perfect blend of aesthetic value and sentiment well worthwhile.

Better yet, go the extra mile by making one yourself. There's no better way to personalize than customizing your creation. Whichever way you choose, take the time to write a personal note expressing how you feel. This can be a quick "I love you" or a detailed affection confession. Use this chance to flirt or pour your heart into a poem. So long as you share your feelings, your partner will cherish the way you've shown them in Week 12 of *52 Love*.

Love Bites

1. How does it feel to receive a personalized card versus an online message or e-card?

_____

_____

_____

2. Do you still own cards from years past? Why or why not?

_____

_____

_____

3. What does the phrase "Hallmark moment" mean to you?

_____

_____

_____

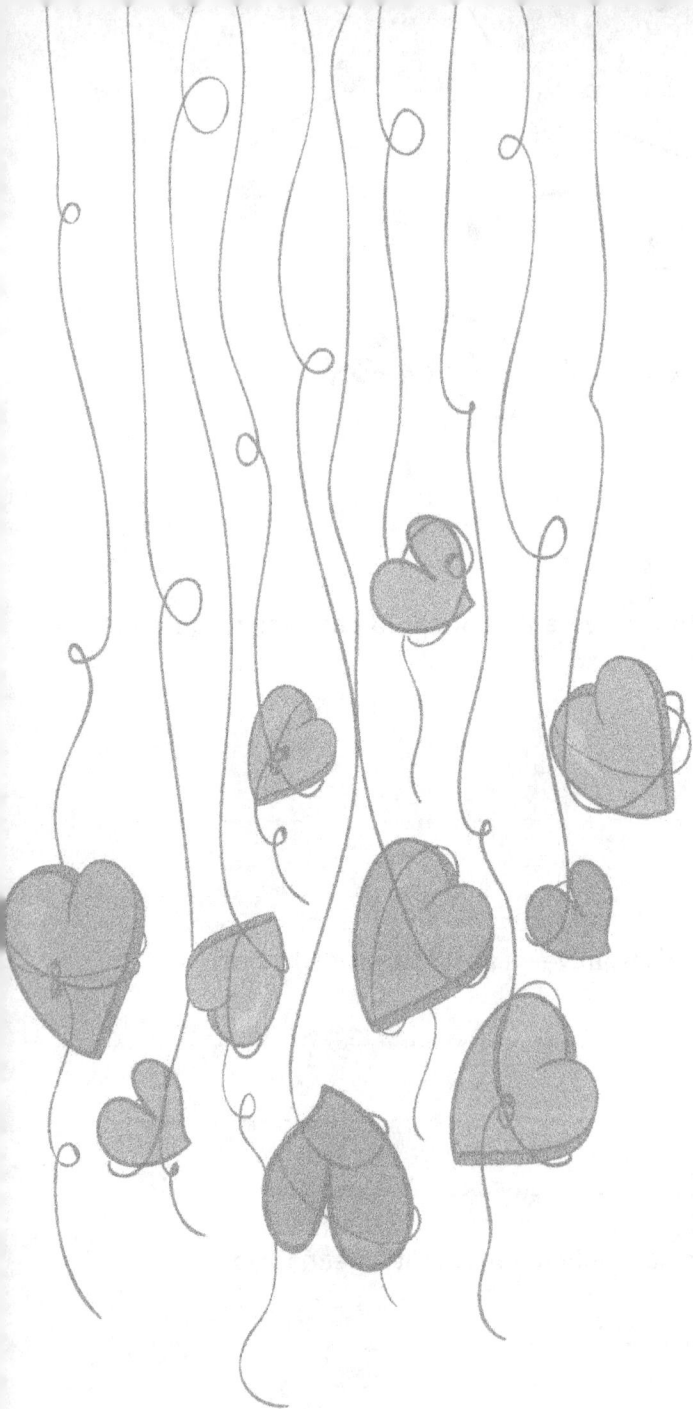

WEEK 13

Biblio Bliss

FOR WEEK 13 OF 52 LOVE, ALLOW ME TO REVISIT MY CHARACTER LUCIAN Blake's bag of tricks. While the main character in my story battles to avoid a romance with the man in question, Lucian shows up on her doorstep and surprises her with a sunset picnic—romantic on its own (and a topic we'll cover in this series). As if his many charms weren't challenging enough to resist, before the light fades, he pulls out a favorite book from his youth and tempts her with the aural pleasure of his mellifluous voice while he reads it to her. Spoiler alert: By the end of the picnic, she is putty in his lap.

Though you may not possess Lucian's cunning finesse, you can show genuine love through the same tactic. Reading to your partner brings you closer as a couple. This shared intimacy taps into your sapiosexual cells by intersecting your intellectual attraction with the physical and emotional draw you have to one another—a powerful experience that will bind you together.

The subject matter doesn't need to be romantic. Read any type of narrative you like. Regardless of the topic, the act of sharing a story together mirrors the closeness of making love and stimulates intimacy.

Reading the story aloud will increase your own enjoyment, too. Slow your pace. Breathe in the experience as your tongue lifts the words from the pages. Appreciate the language choices, the rhythm of the sentences, the flood of emotions now shared with your lover. Emphasize the sensuality of the act by wrapping your arm around her while you read. Snuggle close so she can savor the hum of your voice vibrating through your chest, the thrum of your heartbeat as you share this adventure. The endorphins released from this loving act will help you both sleep better, either from the comforting lull of warm affection or the night of passion your unity inspires.

Love Bites

1. Do you prefer to read to your partner or have your partner read to you? Why?

_____

_____

_____

2. Describe the sensation of feeling the vocal hum through your partner's chest.

_____

_____

_____

3. How does your partner's heartbeat add to this experience?

_____

_____

_____

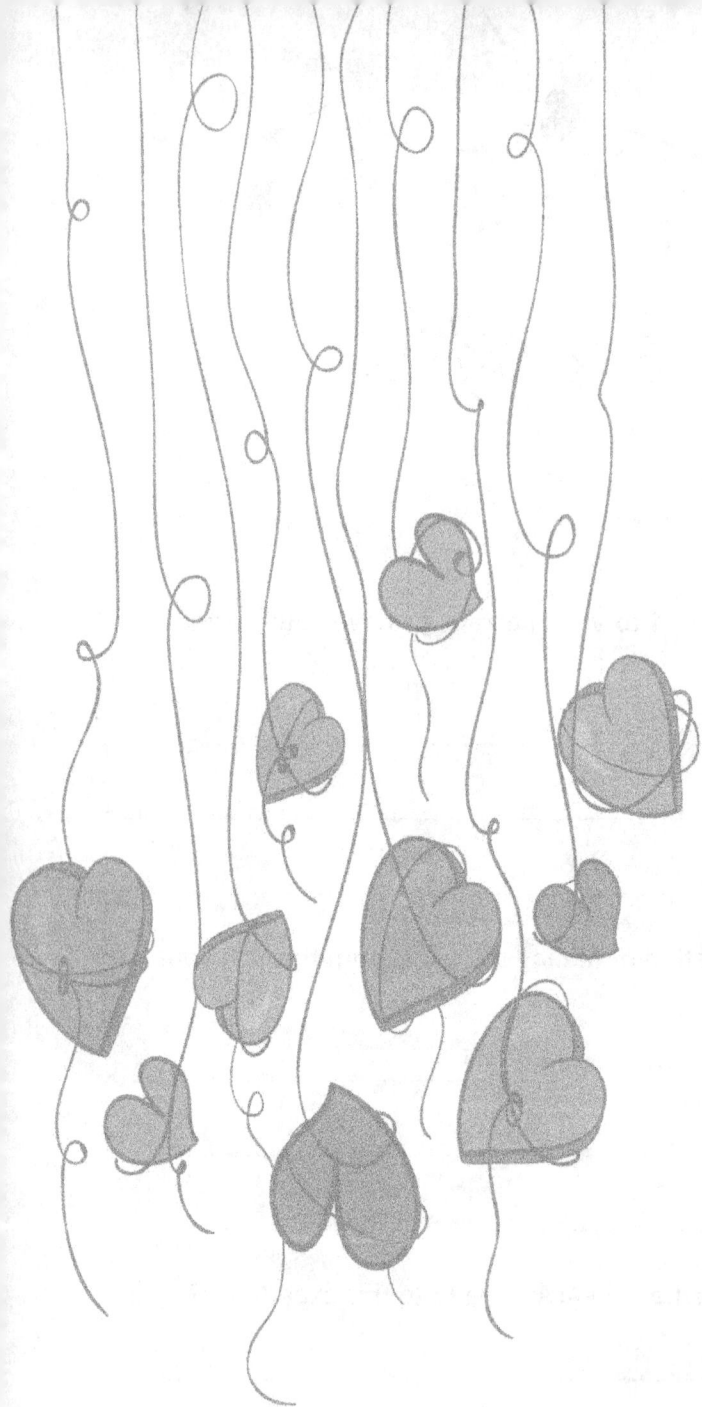

WEEK 14

Let Your Fingers Do the Talking

STRESS GETS TO THE BEST OF US. AND THOUGH DEEP CONVERSATION CAN help with relaxation, try something different for Week 14 of *52 Love*: pamper your partner by massaging a non-sexual body part.

Are there any? No, not really. Any part of your body (especially your mind) can become an instrument for sexual pleasure. The twist for this week's loving gesture is to focus on a part of the body not primarily associated with sex. Trust me. You'll get there.

Non-sexual massage allows you to serve your partner with love—to care for your partner's body. Notice I said non-sexual, not non-sensual. Whether you kneel before your lover to caress tight thighs or straddle his back and rub his bare shoulders, your loving act stimulates affection with this less-lusty form of physical intimacy. Soothe sore muscles with smooth strokes. Delve deeper to relax unwanted tension. Nourish the skin you adore with the rhythmic pulse of your palms. The love you feel will pass from your flesh to his.

On a small scale, this act can enhance an uneventful evening: a scalp massage while he reads a book or a hand massage as you watch your favorite series together. Expand the experience by including more of your lover's body. Wrists. Elbows. Knees. Toes. Explore your partner in ways you haven't. Learn his skin and his reaction to your touch. This wordless communication will speak volumes in a language reserved for only you two.

Bonus points for surprising your sweetie after a shower. Imagine his elation as he dries off with a warm towel and steps into the serene milieu of a personal spa. Prepare soft linens, light candles, and conduct your massage to the score of his favorite relaxing tunes. Heat scented oils to glide over his skin while you caress him, kneading away needless worries with your touch, your time, your service.

Love Bites

1. How can you tell when your partner enjoys the places you're touching?

_____

_____

_____

2. What are your three favorite non-sexual places to be touched?

_____

_____

_____

3. Describe the sensation of your partner's loving caress in those places.

_____

_____

_____

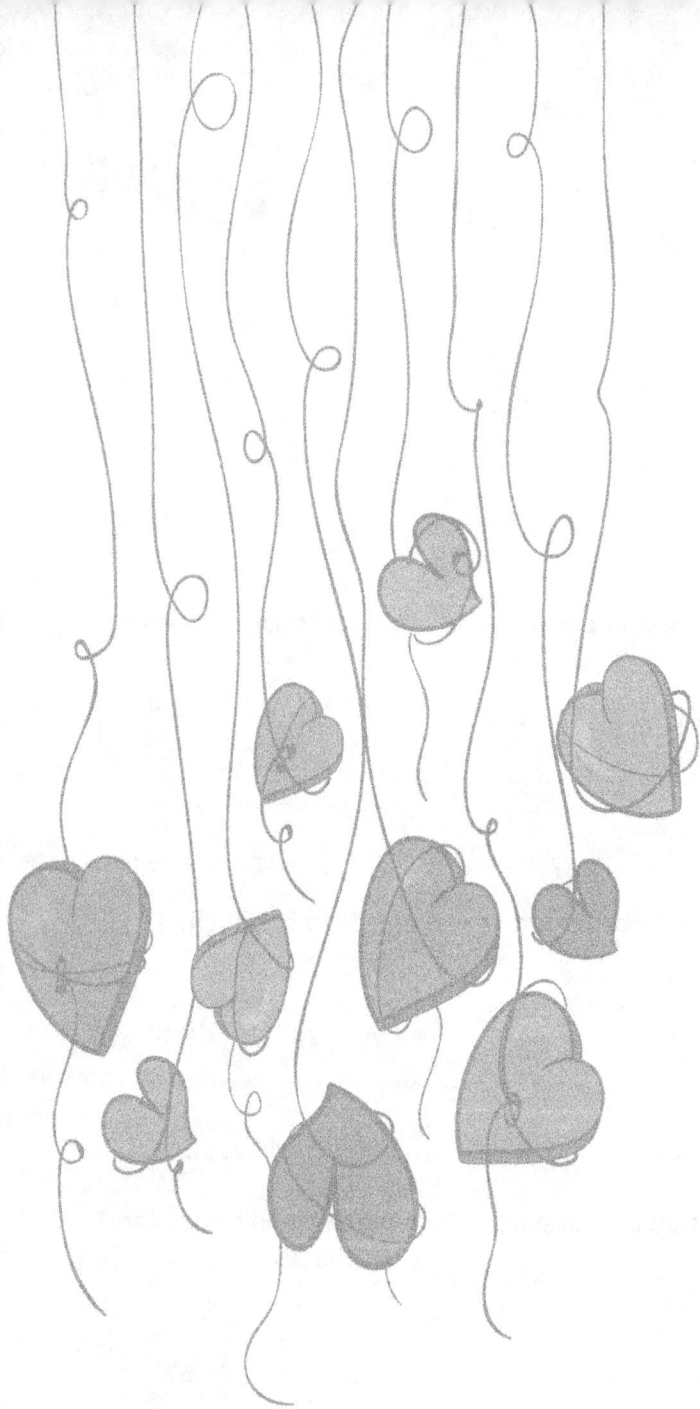

WEEK 15

Pictures Paint a Thousand Affections

COUPLES PHOTOS ARE QUITE FUN, AND I ENCOURAGE YOU TO TRY THEM one day. For Week 15 of *52 Love*, I propose a more intimate approach: create a personal photoshoot for your partner.

Key words: for your *partner*. This is not a boudoir shoot with photos taken for a *recipient*. The focus should be on creating an experience *for your partner*. A photoshoot gives her an excuse to dress up. She can choose an outfit that makes her feel pretty. Sexy. Carefree. Whichever she prefers. The more comfortable she is, the more attractive she'll feel, the more she'll let her inhibitions fly in front of the lens. Letting go of these inhibitions with someone you trust brings you closer together. It binds your love more securely than paying someone to watch you do it.

Avoid the temptation to hire a professional for your shoot. It's about quality time, not quality photos. The pictures merely commemorate your gesture. And though a pro might provide a better product, your loving touch will create better memories.

As a model, I've learned that the photographer sets the tone. The person pointing the lens either mows down the subject with critique and criticism or helps her blossom into vibrant bloom. For a successful shoot, aim for the latter. Be playful. Make her laugh. Recommend silly poses to try. Give her room to try some on her own. Create a safe space to experiment together. In love with a serious girl? Capture her smolder as she broods right into the camera, melting your heart.

Nature creates the best backdrops. Find a remote location free from the world's interruptions, a private spot devoid of other people. A cinematic sunset, a red rock landscape, a sandy beach, a waterfall. Someplace that isolates your adventure from prying eyes.

Posing for a camera may be out of your partner's comfort zone. For many, allowing someone to photograph them truly is a measure of trust. Assure your sweetheart that these photos are for the two of you and that no one else will see them without her permission. Keep this promise. Respect her wishes. Ignore your surging pride at having this beauty in your life. She's involved with you because she loves you, not so you can show her off to your friends.

Remember, this photoshoot declares that you treasure your partner enough to immortalize your affection. Not only will you create a permanent reminder of your good fortune in having snagged such a mate, the two of you will grow closer through the intimacy of the experience. And once you finish—delete bad photos. Celebrate good shots. Enjoy great memories forever.

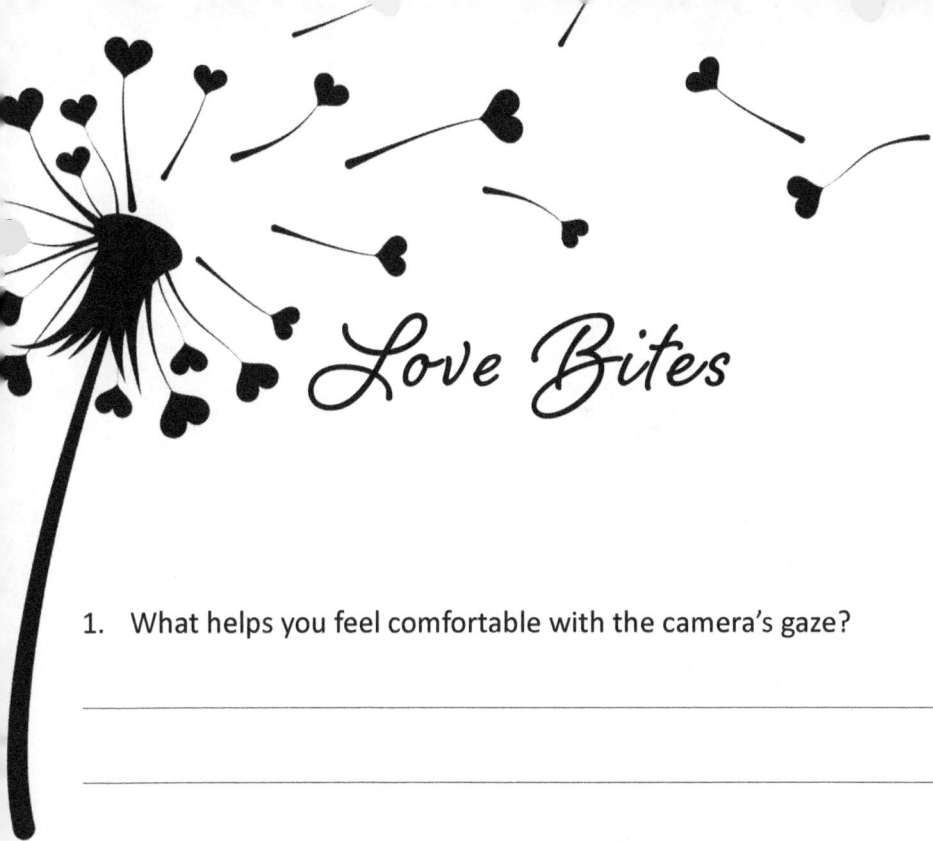

Love Bites

1. What helps you feel comfortable with the camera's gaze?

_____

_____

_____

2. What are some of your favorite photos of each other?

_____

_____

_____

3. What are your favorite photos of yourself? Why?

_____

_____

_____

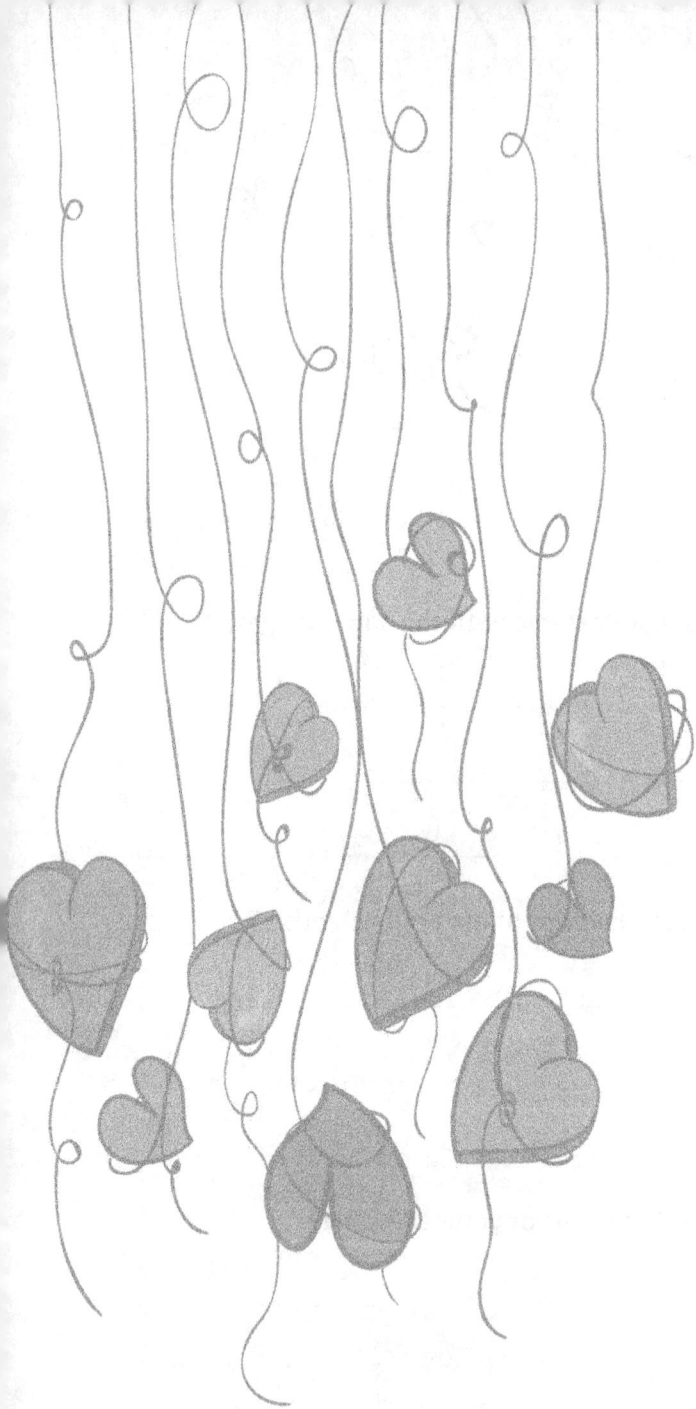

WEEK 16

Learn by Heart

ACQUIRING NEW PROFICIENCIES IS ESSENTIAL TO INDIVIDUAL GROWTH.
For this week's *52 Love* tip, I propose a way for you and your partner
to develop as a healthy, productive couple: Learn a new skill together.

I'm not just talking how to make ceramics *Ghost*-style, although that
would certainly work. There's a whole world of new skills available to
study together. You could give ballroom dancing a whirl or hone the art
of sensual massage. Take archery lessons or develop matching calluses
as you both learn to play guitar. Try your hands at calligraphy, then scribe
loving notes or poems to one another.

Better yet, learn a new language together. Linguistics require frequent practice. When you learn with a partner, you have someone to
help exercise your tongue's proficiency. This type of new skill might
even inspire a vacation to a country that speaks the language. At home

or abroad, it won't be long before you incorporate your new vocabulary into your lovemaking, spicing up an additional area of your romantic life.

Working together will keep you each accountable and provide someone to celebrate your successes. You'll sharpen your skills through repetition and competition. When you learn with a partner, it increases the chances that the new information will stick. You'll each absorb different pieces and learn more concretely when you review them together. And because you can access that review partner so readily, you improve your opportunities to test what you've both learned.

This process creates a sense of teamwork, which builds on the love you share and will carry over to other aspects of your life together. Most importantly, this quality time allows you to learn something new about yourself and about each other which keeps the relationship fresh.

Love Bites

1. What's a skill you've always wanted to learn?

_____

_____

_____

2. What has prevented you from trying it?

_____

_____

_____

3. Do you consider yourself a team player?

_____

_____

_____

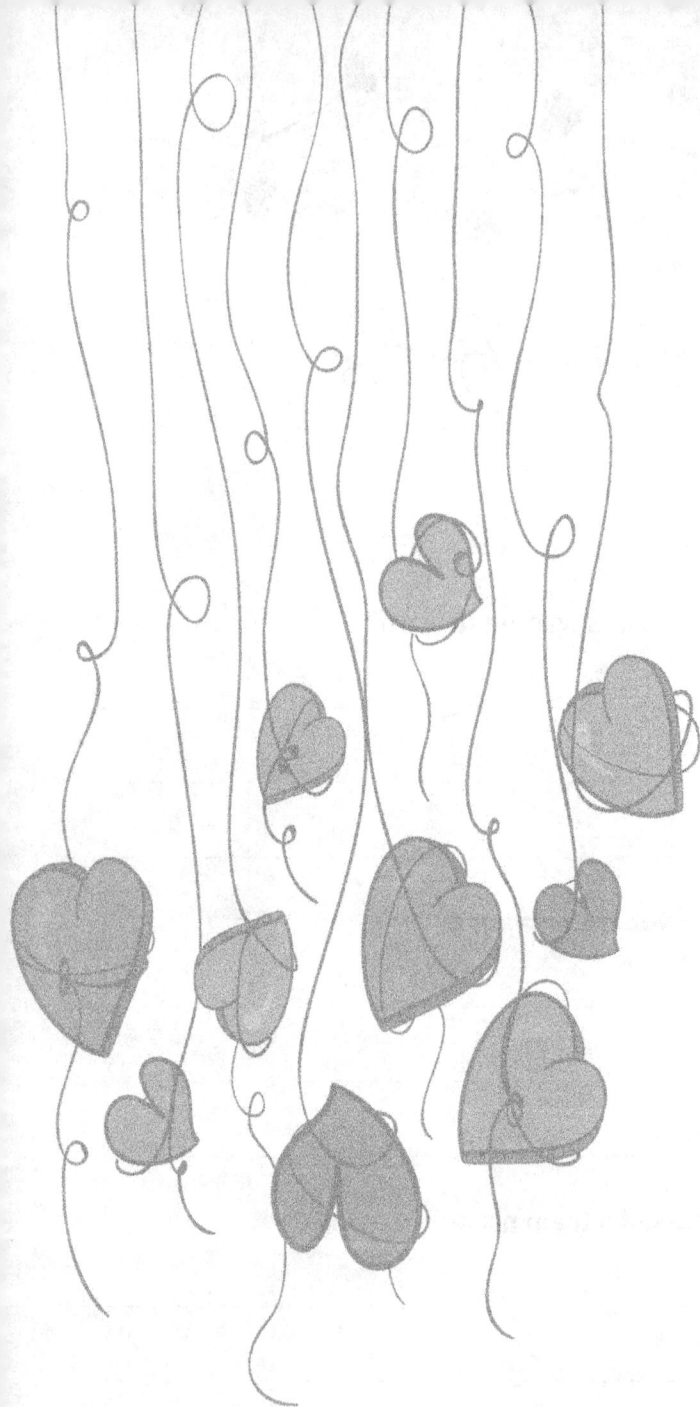

WEEK 17

The Lens of Love

FOR WEEK 17 OF 52 LOVE, IMMORTALIZE YOUR RELATIONSHIP IN THE FORM of a photo collage. Documenting your life through your camera's lens preserves your memories as an expression of your love and allows your partner to relive these moments through your eyes. Considering that "collage" originates from the French word "coller," meaning "to glue," this gift is a perfect choice to make your partner secure in your affections. There's no pressure to complete this within the same week you start. *52 Love* is about the long game.

Feel free to start with existing photos. After that, snap new shots and choose ones deserving of preservation. Go the extra mile by capturing meaningful ordinary moments. As she's reading to your child, when she's gardening in the backyard and the glistening sun bathes her in golden light, while she sips wine from her favorite glass. Bonus points if you snap them without her notice. Different from the glamour of a destination photo shoot like in Week 15, these are shots from everyday life, a candid glimpse at the daily beauty her presence creates.

Relive these loving moments as you assemble your creation. Select high quality images with sharp resolution. Print your shots on good paper. Once you have curated your photos, choose an interesting layout to display them. Find a frame with color and texture that complements your collection. Use the included background or take the time to personalize one.

You can arrange your photos by theme, location, or chronologically—use a multi-frame layout or a single board that you arrange on your own. Or instead of all the photos in one frame, choose two or three frames that hold three or four photos apiece. Your many options are limited only by your creativity and imagination. And if you're crafty enough, when you present this thoughtful gift to your partner, use your camera to capture her expression.

Love Bites

1. Did your family keep photo albums?

_____

_____

_____

2. Do you generally prefer photo collages or multi-frame sets?

_____

_____

_____

3. What do your photos represent to you?

_____

_____

_____

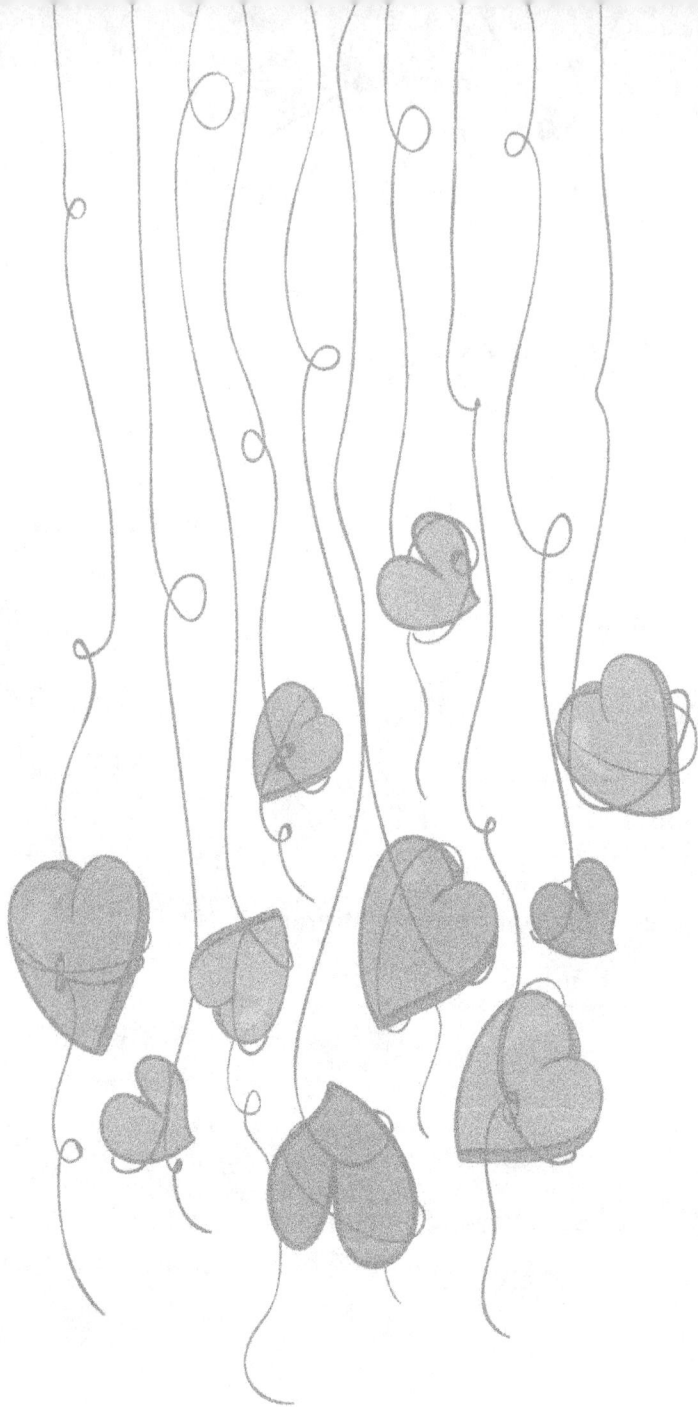

WEEK 18

Get Tantric

WHEN LIVING IN TRYING TIMES, SOME SUFFER FROM LACK OF SOCIAL engagement. Many can't make ends meet. Even if you feel otherwise blessed with your circumstances, the state of the world can manifest into unexpected anxiety. Use Week 18 of *52 Love* to alleviate that unease through tandem prayer.

If you have no experience with joint prayer, it may feel awkward at first. That's okay. Acknowledging this up front will help you overcome the bump by encouraging each other through the process. Much like sexual intimacy, your first time together will stir nervous fears with hopeful anticipation. These moments of shared vulnerability strengthen your bond. Embrace that energy.

Begin by allowing your physical touch to connect you on a spiritual level. Face each other; kneel if you feel comfortable that way. Join hands.

Rest your forehead to his. *Inhale* your shared purpose. *Exhale* your union—warm breaths mingling together within your common space.

Then speak your prayers aloud while maintaining physical contact. Comfort your partner with your words while caressing his skin with your thumbs. Brush the tips of your noses. As your closeness deepens, increase your trust through shared confessions. Confide your fears. Ask for guidance. Speak your gratitudes. Bask in his love while your supportive surge uplifts him. Most importantly, listen to his prayer.

Not spiritually inclined? Think of this as mental and emotional alignment through shared meditation. Create a neurochemical high that transcends your bodies. Release stress and tension by learning to be together on a metaphysical level. Synchronize your breathing. Be comfortable within your partner's space. Make him comfortable within yours. Talk. Listen. Try to understand. In short, find the divine within each other.

Love Bites

1. Separate from religion, do you consider yourself a spiritual person?

_____

_____

_____

2. Did your family pray or meditate together when you were young?

_____

_____

_____

3. Describe the energy involved in connecting this way with your partner.

_____

_____

_____

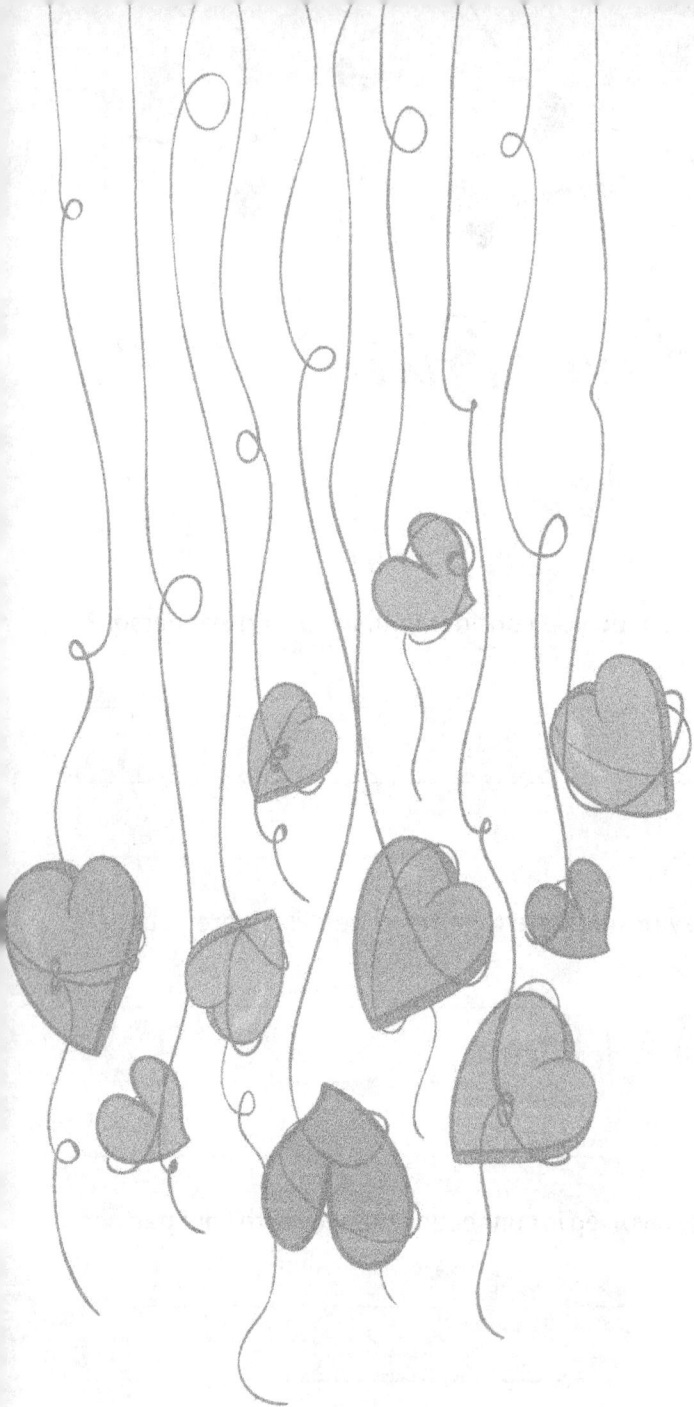

WEEK 19

Lather, Rinse, Romance

IF YOU'VE EVER BENT YOUR NECK TO DIP YOUR HEAD INTO THE BASIN AT a hair salon, you know how amazing it feels for a relative stranger to shampoo and rinse your hair. When done by someone you love, and in the privacy of your own home, it's akin to foreplay. For Week 19 of *52 Love*, wash your partner's hair.

If done with altruistic intentions, this act can reward you as much as your partner. Service strengthens your bond. You may recall an episode of *Grey's Anatomy* where Meredith had just escaped a bomb's explosion. Her friends joined her in the shower to wash away what they could of the trauma with their bare hands. They gave freely and the experience drew them closer. Think of this experience as a way to serve your lover. Your goal is to clean her hair, scrub her scalp, and make her feel loved in the process.

For the purpose of this exercise, we'll assume you're sharing a shower. Evocative scents and textures enhance the romance. Instead of her usual shampoo, consider a brand with exotic essential oils to add an element of luxury. Adjust the water to a safe temperature. Then, clasp your partner's forearm, turn it over in your hands, and test the water together. Once you have her preferred pressure and temperature, gently dip her head into the water. Saturate her hair down to the scalp. Pay attention as some heads of hair take longer to penetrate than others.

Once the area is thoroughly wet, squeeze enough shampoo into your palm to work up a good froth. Lather the slick foam through her hair thoroughly. This is a great opportunity to incorporate the massage tips from Week 14. Remember the temples and nape of the neck. Spend extra time at the roots to remove buildup from oils, sweat, dirt, and even makeup.

Curly hair takes extra care. Tender heads and tangles can kill the mood. Work one section at a time using gentle strokes to prevent knots and snagging. Avoid circular swirling. Aim for downward motions at a slow, rhythmic pace, gradually move your fingers deeper as you go.

Each head of hair is unique. When in doubt about what to do, ask. Use this experience to start a dialogue about what she likes and where she likes it, not to mention how she wants you to do it. Your comfort with these discussions will likely translate to greater intimacy in other areas.

This type of physical contact arouses endorphins. Your loving act isn't meant as a prelude to sex, yet the sensual pleasure provoked by your fingertips may lead there. Let that be her call. Your job is to keep your hands where she wants them during this deeply caring gesture. Even if it remains chaste, seeing the ecstasy in your partner's face will bring you pleasure, too.

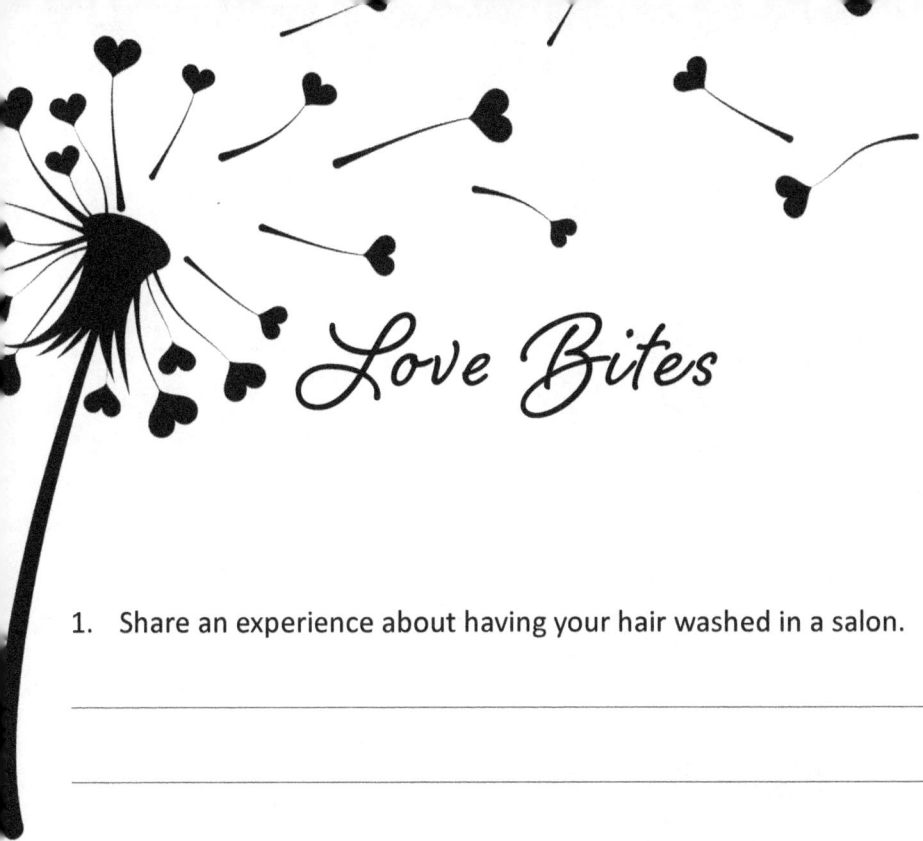

Love Bites

1. Share an experience about having your hair washed in a salon.

_____

_____

_____

2. What is your preferred temperature for hair-washing?

_____

_____

_____

3. Does having your hair washed stimulate you, relax you, or both?

_____

_____

_____

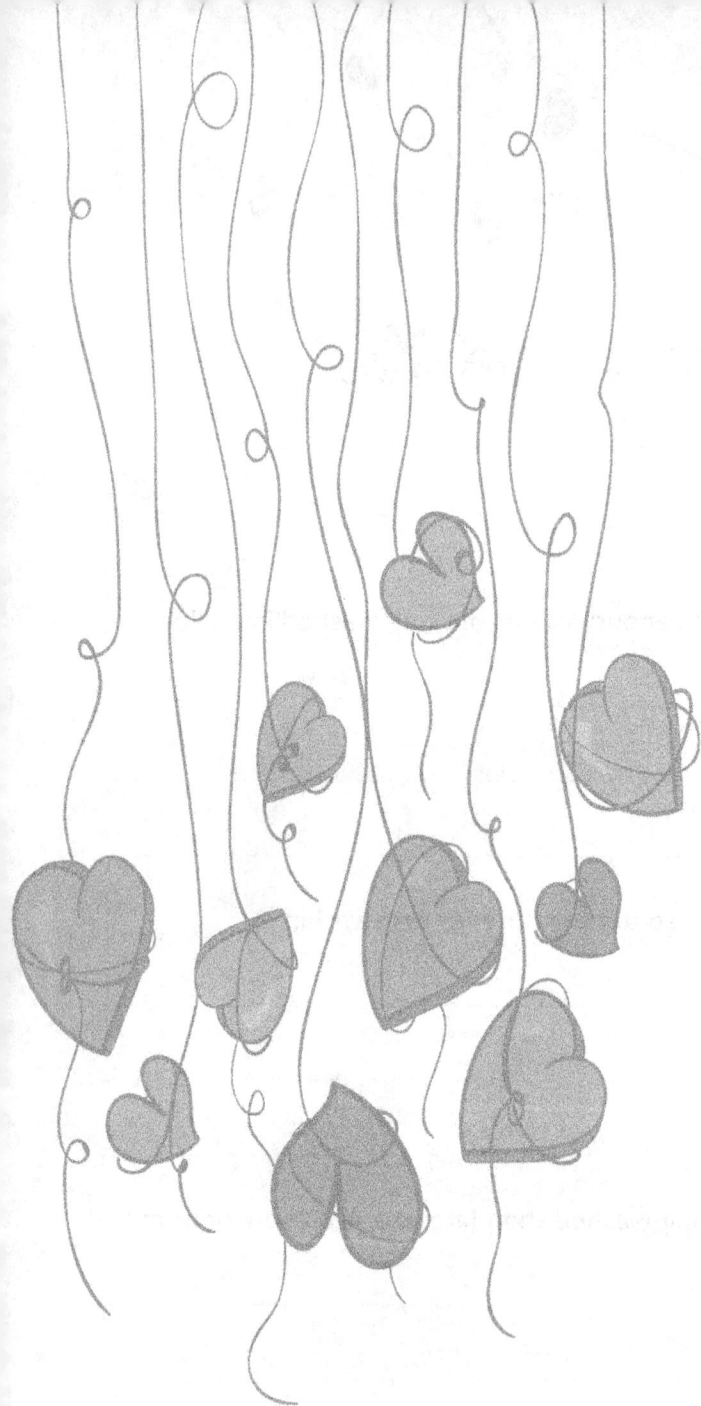

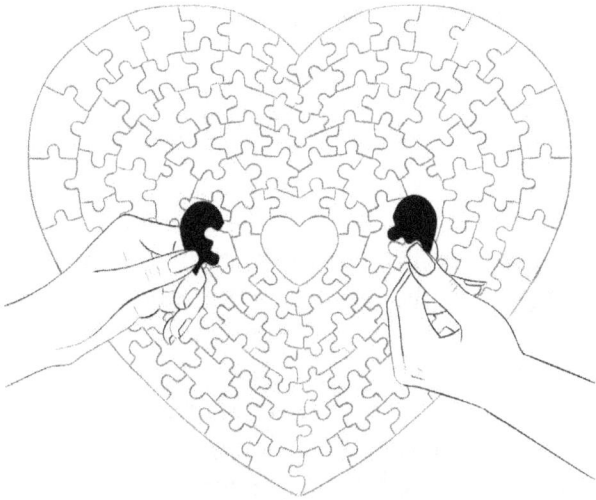

WEEK 20

Pieced Together Peace

THE PANDEMIC INSPIRED A ROBUST RESURGENCE IN INDOOR ACTIVITIES.
If your mind flew to the same naughty thought as mine, this week's *52 Love* suggestion may perplex you. Rather than bedroom gymnastics, I recommend something that works well without the need to undress: a complex jigsaw puzzle. As with most of my tips, clothing is optional.

Jigsaw puzzles offer a chance to break from binge-watching, disengage from the digital world, and escape external stressors. Unplugging from screens and devices is important for mental health. With that in mind, clear a spot for two, lead your partner to the playing field, spread your pieces, and relax as you join them together.

Solving puzzles improves mental and physical health. It increases concentration while keeping your brain busy and stimulated, free from negative input. Puzzle-solving provides a sense of restoring order to the chaos we're facing in our lives, a sense of accomplishment when so little is in our control.

Alone, this small victory can work wonders on our psyches. Together it builds the foundation for a strong partnership. Just as puzzles improve your memory by reinforcing the existing connections between your brain cells, joint puzzle play reinforces the connections between you and your partner.

Solving a jigsaw puzzle engages both the intuitive and creative sides of your brain. While you improve your attention span and problem-solving skills, you sharpen your brains as a couple. Subsequently, this exercise will help strengthen your bond as a problem-solving team.

A larger puzzle may last for days, allowing you to connect throughout the week. Use this one-on-one time to encourage creativity and communication. Chat about childhood memories, current challenges, or future plans. See where the conversation leads you. If there are elusive pieces, employ a bit of healthy competition while you work toward the same goal. No losers in this game.

This focused activity will serve as a stress-reliever that keeps you fully in the moment. Working toward a common goal strengthens you and your partner as a team. Sit side by side, across from each other, or plant yourself in his lap. The point is, you're working together. Everyday worries will evaporate as you meditate on your joint task. Soon, peace and tranquility will replace the day's concerns and draw you closer. And like playing games in Week 6, you can add a sexy twist by removing clothing at each completed milestone, which may lead to those other robust indoor activities.

Love Bites

1. When you were growing up, did you and your family assemble puzzles together?

_____

_____

_____

2. In terms of pieces, what's the biggest puzzle you've ever completed?

_____

_____

_____

3. Do you tend to find puzzles intimidating or an inviting challenge?

_____

_____

_____

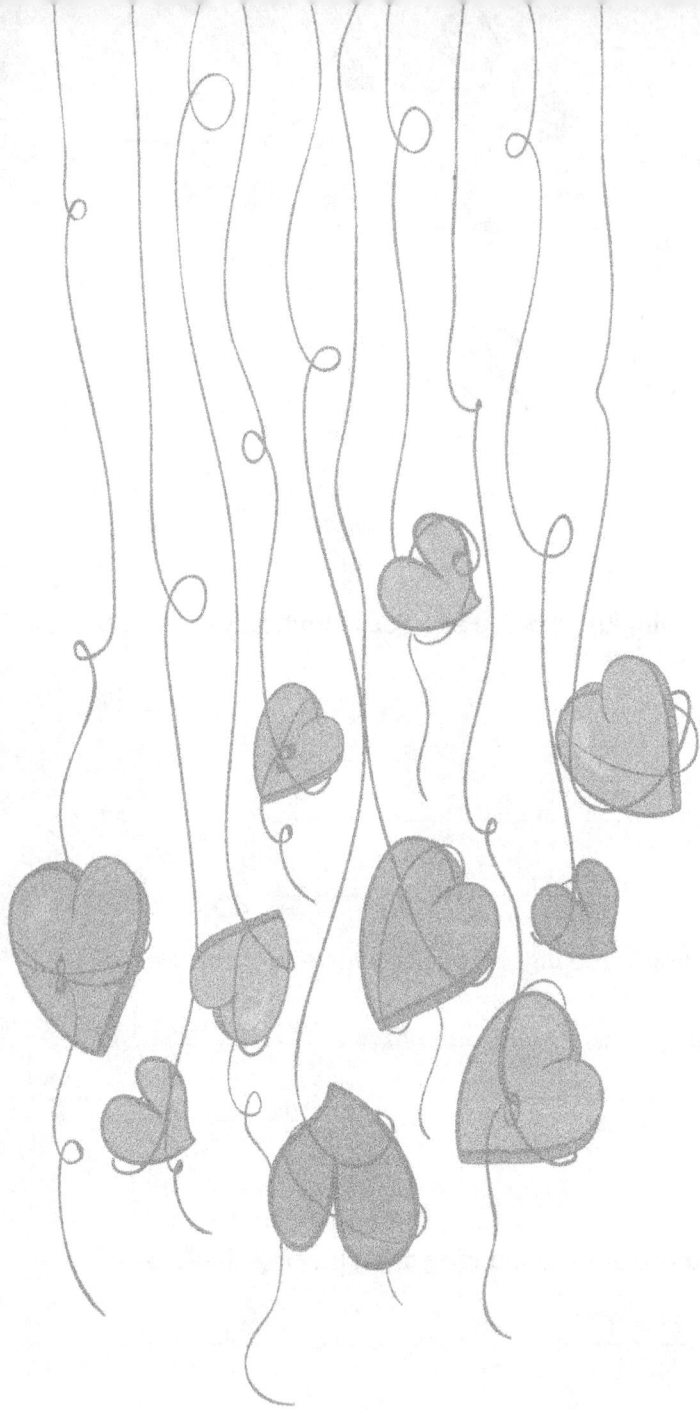

WEEK 21

Journal Your Journey

COMMUNICATION IS KEY TO BUILDING A SOLID RELATIONSHIP. WRITING encourages you to explore your language; writing about your relationship allows you to explore each other. For Week 21 of *52 Love*, start a couple's journal as a proactive approach to strengthening your bond.

The inspiration for this week's post comes from a family member. In the early stages of their relationship, she and her partner wrote in a shared journal when they were apart because they missed each other. Once they moved in together, she would take it to school if she had a challenging week that didn't allow time to get worries off her chest. He would do the same when work was stressful. This couple, now married, already has a strong foundation of sharing and communication.

No matter what stage you and your partner face in your journey, a joint journal empowers you to record your experiences and tackle life's greatest challenges. Through journaling, you and your partner can share joys, thoughts, dreams, disappointments, hopes, concerns, and desires. This practice helps you relive relationship highlights or devote extra attention to challenges you need to address.

Some guidelines to keep in mind: Before you begin this journal, establish ground rules. Determine how frequently you would both like to write, be it every day, weekly, or simply when inspiration strikes. Do you want to use different colored ink to spot each other's entries? Going in with the same expectations curbs disappointment and avoids unnecessary pressure.

Journaling has a calming effect that helps you let go of negative thoughts. Letting go of negativity leads to a happier, healthier relationship. Simply writing about your troubles will ease your mind, which allows you to communicate better when the two of you discuss those troubles. Both of you should write freely, without fear of judgment. Treat your partner's entries with respect. Avoid dismissing her concerns or feelings about them. Remind her of her strengths in the situations she presents and that you have her back no matter what. This improved emotional and physical health will help you fight battles outside of your journal.

Regardless of how much you love someone, there will be times when you upset each other. Your journal offers a path to express those frustrations in a constructive manner. First, release your pent-up negative emotions with your raw, honest thoughts. Then use your journal to view the negative experiences as obstacles to overcome together.

When discussing frustration with each other, stick to "I" statements and steer clear of accusatory language. The goal is to express your feelings and open a constructive dialogue. If your partner confides that something you do causes her anxiety, the journal enables you to examine that behavior and address the challenge with clear lines of communication, free from judgment. No punishments for what is written. Instead, see those unhappy verses for what they are—a doorway toward relationship growth.

Focus on open intimacy, not perfection. When freewriting, you may misspell a word or articulate your point through stream of consciousness. Forgive each other these errors and focus on your goals. Your journal is sacred intel, not public work meant for publication. When what is written between the two of you stays between the two of you, couples journaling becomes a powerful means to strengthen your relationship and ultimately foster better communication.

Sharing a journal can provide an easier way to start conversations you may need to have because you are thinking more about your words and are less emotional after writing. Sometimes initiating these conversations in person can be difficult. If you read your partner's entries with empathy and understanding, your new insight can spark vital and constructive discussions while building a trusting relationship.

A couple's journal also offers opportunity to reinforce the positive by recording memories and supporting one another. Sometimes you may want to remind your partner that you love her and what is happening in your life is making you happy. Use the journal to show enthusiasm for the things you love about her. Express those gratitudes we discussed in Week 11. Record a couple's bucket list. Share small memories she may not realize were important to you. If you feel it's significant, then she'll want to know.

Over time, the journal will help you and your partner learn more about yourselves, each other, and your relationship. Share things you want her to know about you. What are you too self-conscious to say aloud? Embrace the chance to discover more about each other.

Once the journal becomes a relationship staple, you may enjoy having that document of your journey to reread later. You and your partner can relive sentimental entries. Revisit the journal when in need of encouragement. Your private couples journal holds the inner workings of your relationship. Review segments as reminders for what's important to you both and anticipate what is still to come.

Love Bites

1. Which topics are easier to communicate in writing as opposed to speaking them aloud?

_____

_____

_____

2. Which topics would you rather say than write?

_____

_____

_____

3. Have you ever kept a personal journal or diary? If so, what age did you start?

_____

_____

_____

WEEK 22

The Way to His Heart

COOKING CAN OFTEN FEEL LIKE A CHORE. YET BE IT GRAND CELEBRATIONS, playful picnics, or family mealtime, food brings people together. Instead of dreading this fundamental staple, turn it into a bonding experience by seasoning your relationship with the ingredients for a long, loving partnership. For Week 22 of *52 Love*, cook a meal with your partner.

Most rate the ability to cook as highly attractive. Even if cooking isn't your forte, the act of trying marks you as an attractive mate. If a novice, you produce humorous memories. If a pro, that confident competence kindles intimacy in and out of the kitchen.

Preparing meals together connects you on a deeper level. Working as a team builds trust. Creating something together requires cooperation. When you rely on each other and work toward a common goal, it solidifies the notion that the two of you have a partnership. Whether you choose one dish and share the tasks or divide multiple dishes between you, being able to stay on the same page when preparing a recipe speaks well for your ability to stay on the same page as a couple. Even making something as simple as grilled cheese sandwiches with tomato soup inspires a shared sense of satisfaction far more gratifying than going it alone.

Cooking together fosters communication skills. For many couples, kitchen duties are split between meal prep and cleaning. Although this is a fair division of chores, it equates to separated bodies. Rather than spending that time apart as you each work independently, share that time together. Chat about the day, plans for the week, or treasured memories from childhood. Whether tossing a simple salad or concocting a five-course meal, embrace this chance to connect over one-on-one time in the kitchen.

In Week 16, we covered how sharing personal development with your partner strengthens your relationship. When cooking together, you also learn from each other. You each bring different skills to the table. Nobody is competing. Rather than argue about whose method is best, experiment with each other's preferences. Cultivate an environment that stimulates creativity. Meld each other's ideas into delicious cuisine emblematic of the team who built it.

Cooking can be a sensuous activity. Creativity stimulates your senses. Channel that energy to get his blood pumping in the tight confines of your kitchen. Have fun during downtime. While waiting for water to boil, dance to a favorite song. Strip tease as the meat simmers. Feed him unused ingredients by hand. Mix in a little saucy flirting, combined with some spicy wordplay, and your skillet won't be the only thing sizzling in the kitchen.

Once your meal is on the table, enjoy the succulent reward together. Pour two glasses of wine and continue date night over dinner conversation. Feed your partner morsels from your plate. Whether your kitchen tales consist of hilarious mistakes or spectacular culinary creations, the meals you prepare together will become linked to the emotions that accompany the experience. Build memories seasoned with the love and care that went into preparing your meal.

Love Bites

1. What are some favorite memories of when food brought people together?

_____

_____

_____

2. What meals did you help make with your family when you were a child?

_____

_____

_____

3. What do you appreciate most about cooking with your partner?

_____

_____

_____

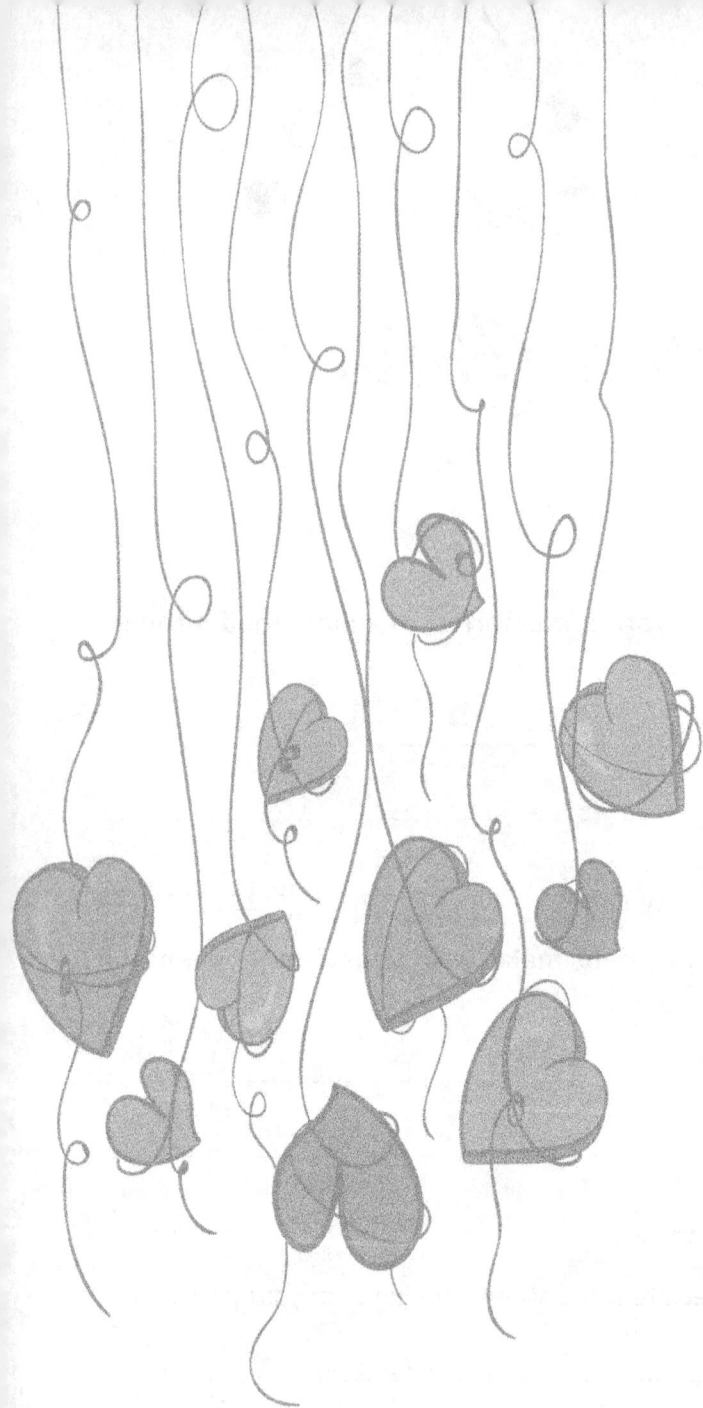

WEEK 23

Compassionate Companionship

VOLUNTEERING TOGETHER IS A WONDERFUL WAY TO BOND WITH YOUR partner. Flexing empathetic muscles helps with understanding other people's needs and struggles. That generosity strengthens you as a person, which translates to you becoming a better mate. When you volunteer together, you'll see the best in each other and ultimately feel better about yourself and your partner. Embrace the chance to see your partner's altruistic side. Show her yours. No matter the cause you support, develop those useful skills and apply them to each other.

Building compassion builds companionship. Create memorable experiences when volunteering together. The act of helping others releases oxytocin. Increase your pleasure by experiencing that release together. It's not the reason to serve others, but it's an inevitable byproduct of the experience. Enjoy those positive vibes together. Whether the invigoration from your volunteer work at the local wolf sanctuary or the shared victory when a child you've mentored crosses the finish line at the Special Olympics, your charitable time will manifest into treasured memories. Through these shared, meaningful experiences, your partnership will grow stronger and more connected.

Helping others, especially when feeling down yourself, offers a boost to your own morale and wellbeing. Moreover, if you point that charitable heart toward a cause near and dear to your partner, you will help others *and* strengthen your relationship. Learn about her passions and fight for her causes. Whether that means you donate funds to World Wildlife Fund, organize a donation drive for homeless teens, or march on the front lines at a protest, your actions prove that you stand united with her and that things that matter to her also matter to you.

Eventually, volunteering together will establish an environment of appreciation in your relationship and allow you to grow into better versions of yourselves. Witnessing other people's challenges can humble you and your partner. Use that humility to boost your gratitude for the blessings in your life. Reinforce those shared values by counting your blessings together. Let it foster a philosophy of kindness between you. Not only you as a couple, but the plural you and the world.

Love Bites

1. What are three causes that speak to you?

_____

_____

_____

2. How does it feel when you donate time versus money?

_____

_____

_____

3. When did giving back to community register as important in your life?

_____

_____

_____

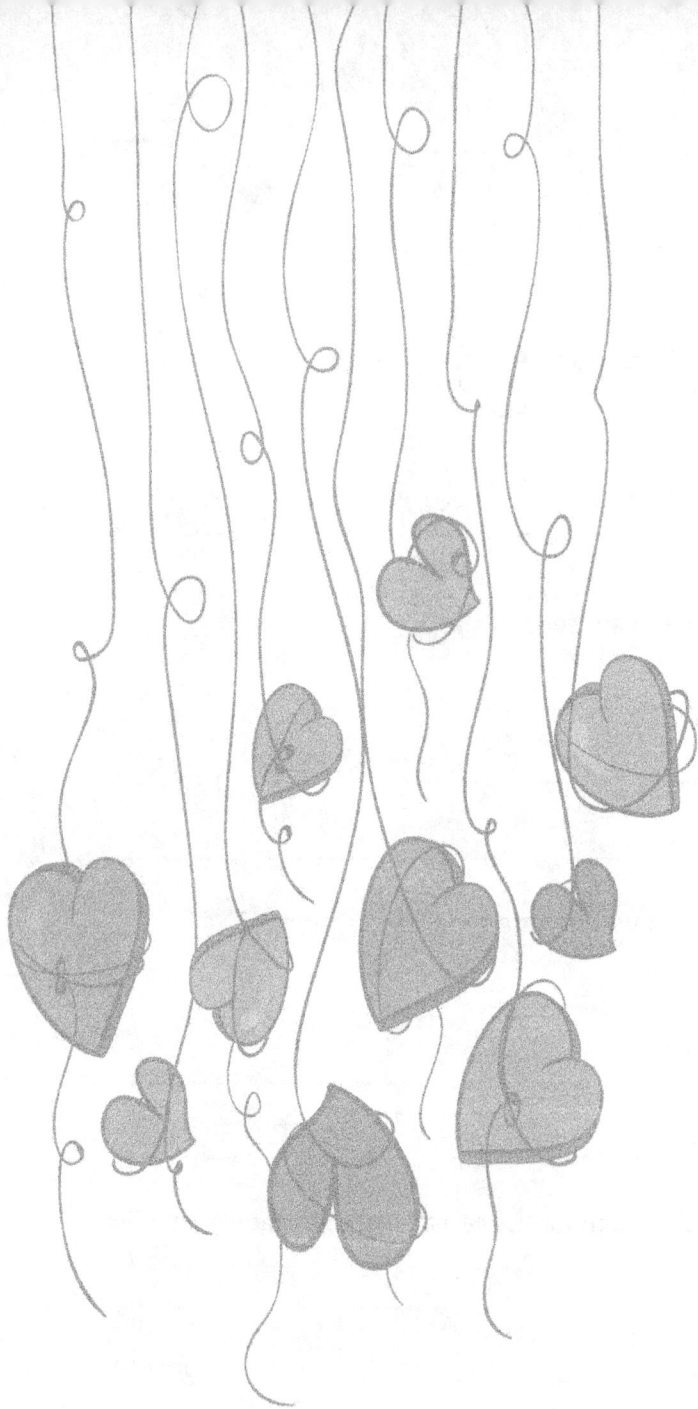

WEEK 24

Keep that Love Machine Humming

CAR-WASHING IS AN IMPORTANT, TIME-CONSUMING TASK. IT ISN'T A NEED, but it feels like one. Yet no matter the method, I grumble through the car-washing process. At a commercial facility, the chairs in the waiting area are dirty, the floor is sticky, and the combination of grease, chemicals, and industrial cleaner nauseates me. The wait steals precious time from chores, responsibilities, or activities I actually enjoy. Using the drive-through isn't much better. It saves time, but the interior stays dirty and the exterior only gets cleanish.

Imagine my delight when I find that this task was handled for me. Sparkling dashboard, conditioned seats, vacuumed floors, smudge-free mats—all without having to leave my home. Now imagine your partner's appreciation should you handle it for him.

Cleaning your partner's vehicle is a way to show him love in a practical way. Depending on his preference, you could run it through the wash and clean the interior on your own or sit through the commercial wash for him. Either way, you free up his time to spend elsewhere and remind him that you love him.

For some, car-washing is an endeavor they'd prefer to experience first-hand rather than relinquish to someone else. Instead of hijacking the task, help him with the workload. Someone who chooses to clean a car by hand is likely particular about the method and result. You're undertaking this task to get closer, not argue about perceived OCD. It's his car. You're showing him love. Wash it his way. Does he insist on a specific order for which segments to tackle? Does he prefer concentric circles for applying wax? Follow the order and his instructions, even if you find them ridiculous. It's not the car-washing that's important to you. It's him.

If you're feeling especially frisky, get playful with it. Slip into your shortest cut-offs and don a white T-shirt to play out the sudsy car-washing fantasy. Tease him with naughty talk while you spritz him with the hose. Regardless of your own gender, this experience will cling to him like the see-through shirt you "accidentally" soaked. And once his vehicle is pristine and clean, you can help each other out of those wet clothes.

Love Bites

1. How frequently do you wash your vehicle?

_____

_____

_____

2. Do you enjoy washing your vehicle by hand, or would you prefer to take it to a professional cleaner?

_____

_____

_____

3. What are your favorite associations with a clean car?

_____

_____

_____

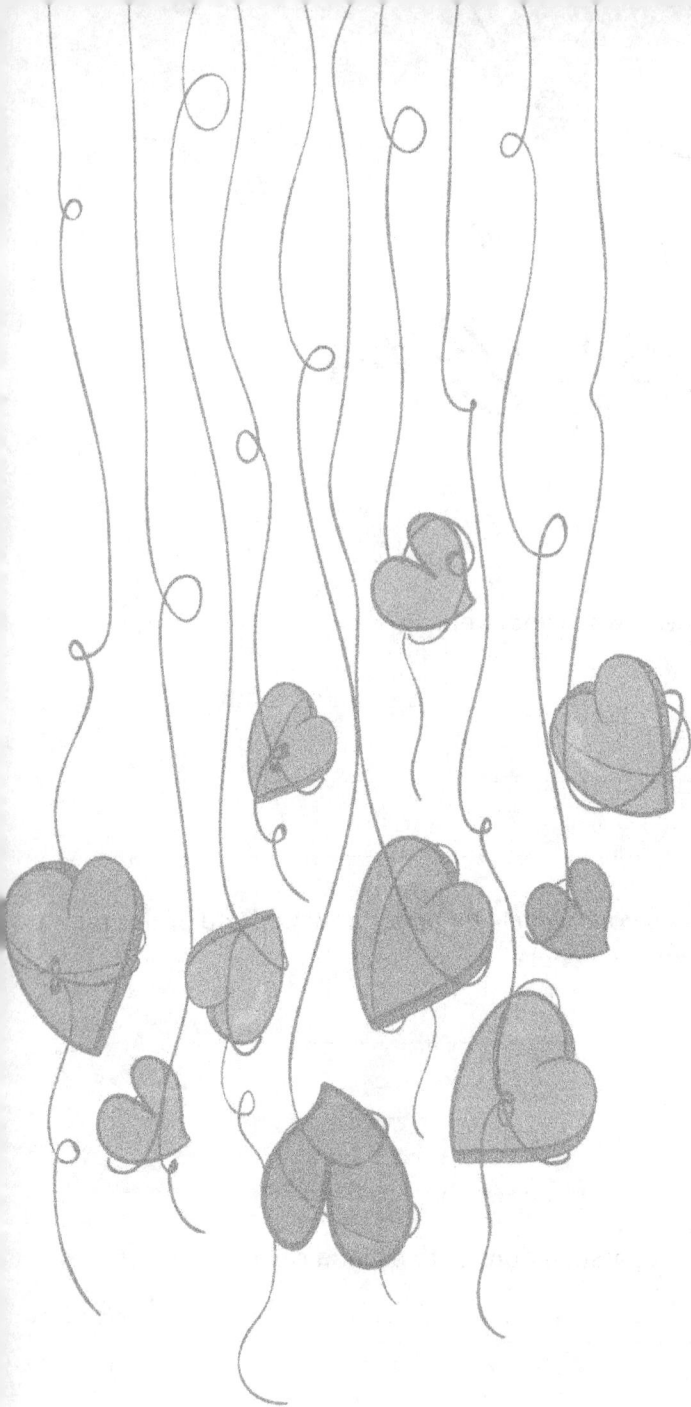

WEEK 25

Fall through the Windows to the Soul

NICOLA YOON'S *THE SUN IS ALSO A STAR* TAUGHT ME THAT FOUR SILENT minutes can ignite a spark between people. That lesson prompted this week's tip. If looking into a stranger's eyes for four minutes makes you fall in love, consider how it can increase intimacy between existing lovers. For Week 25 of *52 Love,* find a quiet spot, silence notifications, and gaze into your partner's eyes for four minutes.

Constant eye contact may sound daunting. In our digital point-and-click world, four minutes is a long time to focus on anything, let alone stare at someone without talking. At first, your emotional discomfort may manifest in physical ticks. This isn't a staring contest. It's acceptable to blink. It's okay to laugh, too. Expect a few outbursts of nervous smiling until you settle in together.

Because you care more about what she thinks of you, staring into your partner's eyes may be more challenging than staring into a stranger's. Not only are you looking at your partner, you are allowing her to see you. Similar to tandem prayer, this experience opens the door to shared vulnerability. So long as you take the exercise seriously—no funny faces— you can ride those awkward waves together.

Focused eye contact stimulates affection. Once you get past the initial strangeness, you and your partner will be open and connected to one another. The quiet moments might trigger memories from your time together or inspire new appreciation for the sparkle shining your way. Eye contact can also cause arousal. Whatever your response, channel those thoughts and emotions into a four-minute reminder to treasure your partner and appreciate her presence in your life.

This focused time invites you and your partner to forge a tighter bond and strengthen your connection. Afterward, you can discuss how you felt during the four minutes. Better yet, *show* your partner how you feel now.

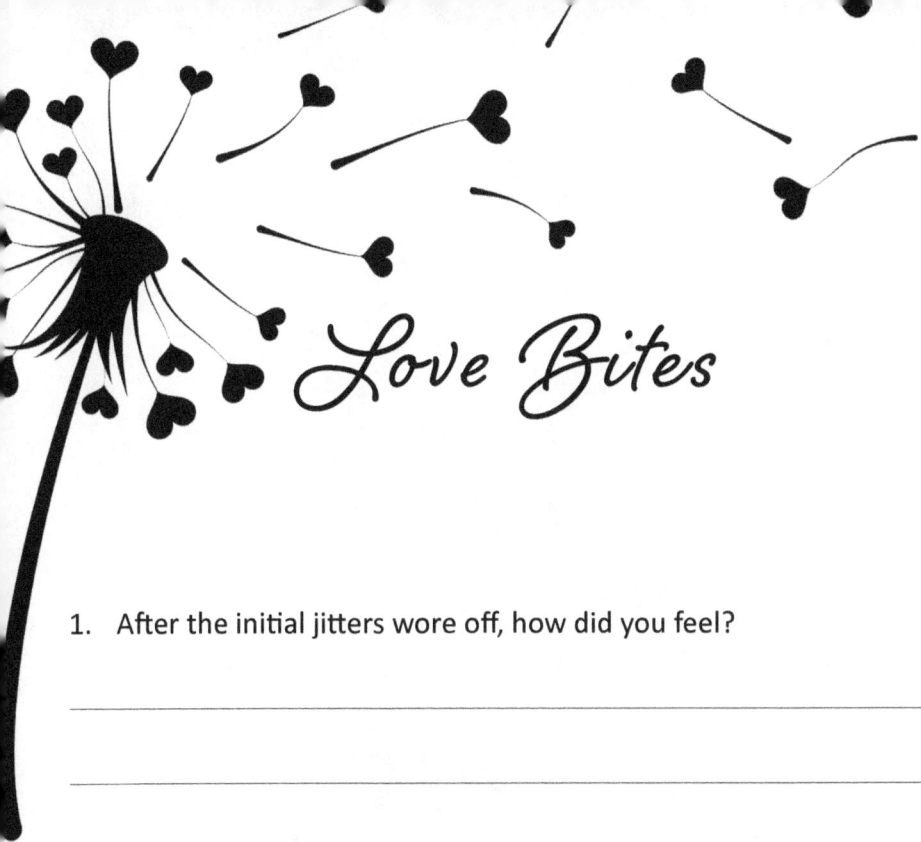

Love Bites

1. After the initial jitters wore off, how did you feel?

   _____

   _____

   _____

2. Did you discover anything new about your partner's eye color?

   _____

   _____

   _____

3. After this experience, why do you think people say eyes are the windows to the soul?

   _____

   _____

   _____

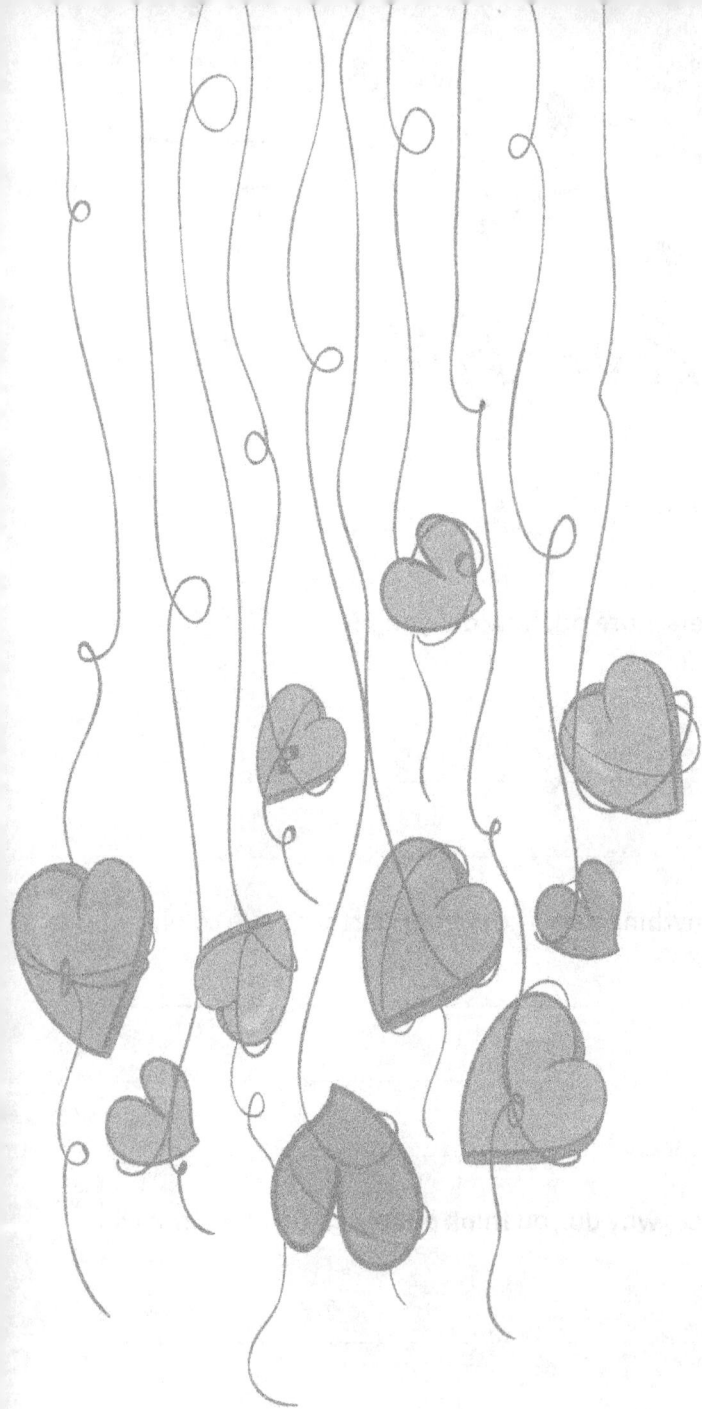

WEEK 26

Be A Doll

AS WE REACH THE HALF-WAY POINT FOR 52 LOVE, LET'S REFLECT ON HOW we've shown our partners affection this year. We've held hands, gazed into each other's eyes, and listened to one another. Most *52 Love* tips focused on one person's efforts. This week's suggestion may challenge you both equally.

For Week 26, let your partner dress you for a shared outing. This venture will be riskier for some than others. We aren't all blessed with style fashionistas for partners. You may fear he'll pair clashing items or worry he'll dress you in something too sexy to leave the house—he does love the way you look in nothing but his old gym shirt. Regardless of how you feel about the ensemble he chooses, maintain your poker face. Surrender to your partner's whims. This isn't about yielding power. It's about sharing the experience and learning what your partner likes.

Whatever his choice, allowing this push out of your comfort zone is part of the deal.

This may be scary for him, too. He won't want to disappoint you and may feel out of his depths. Resist the urge to make suggestions. Wearing what he chooses reveals your trust in his competence, which strengthens your bond as a couple. It's all connected. You open the door to him. In accepting what he brings without judgment, you increase his trust and affection for you.

It may help to set some ground rules. Your partner can't ask you to leave the house in something that breaks public indecency laws. Stay home if he picks the gym shirt. And you should be able to voice if something causes pain or physical discomfort (itchy, too hot or cold for the season). Stay silent if it only discomforts your vanity. If you're feeling particularly vulnerable with your partner's selection, ask his reason for the choice. When asked without criticism, the question may receive an answer that inspires pride, not embarrassment.

Have faith. Your partner may surprise you. He might retrieve an old forgotten item from the back of your closet or pair typically mismatched patterns with an impressive flair of style. Your partner may reveal a strong desire for skin-tight, black, and shiny. Or you may learn he leans toward bright colors, lacy tops, or polka dot bow ties. Even if it's not attractive to you, wear the outfit with pride. Remember, you look great to him.

Embrace the confidence boost from knowing the most important person in your world thinks you're a knockout today. As you saunter toward the eyes of the public, ignore your increased sense of self-awareness, and instead, focus on your partner's fixation on you as he parades past your perceived paparazzi with his personal dress-up doll on his arm. After an evening of him gazing at you, eyes full of love and admiration, you may walk away from this experiment with the confidence to take more risks with your wardrobe. You'll certainly take more risks with him.

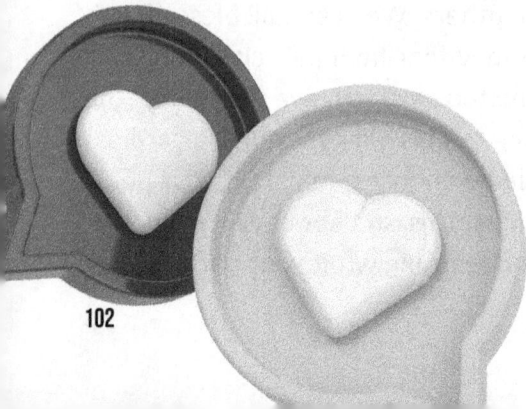

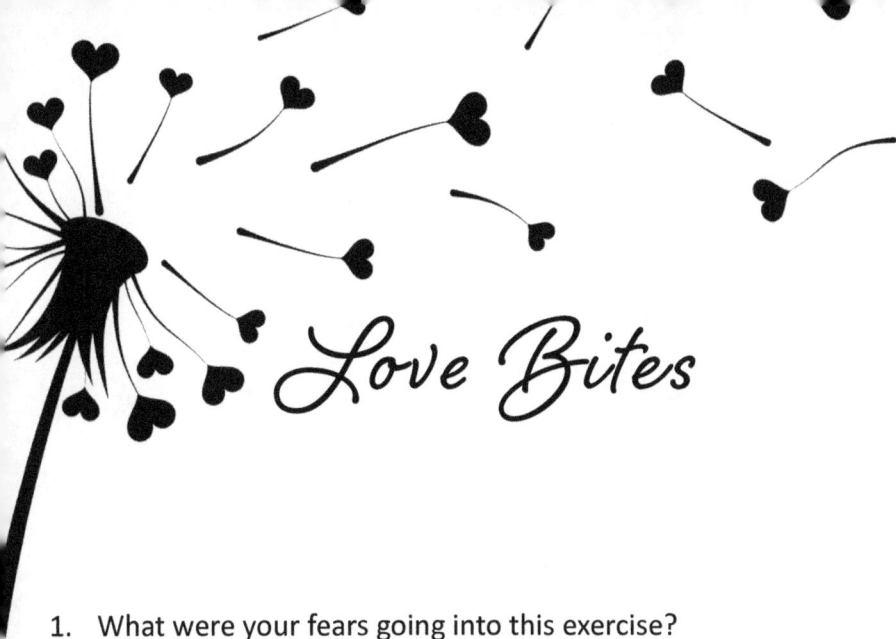

Love Bites

1. What were your fears going into this exercise?

_____

_____

_____

2. If your styles clashed, did you do a good job of handling it?

_____

_____

_____

3. What would you do differently if you repeated the exercise?

_____

_____

_____

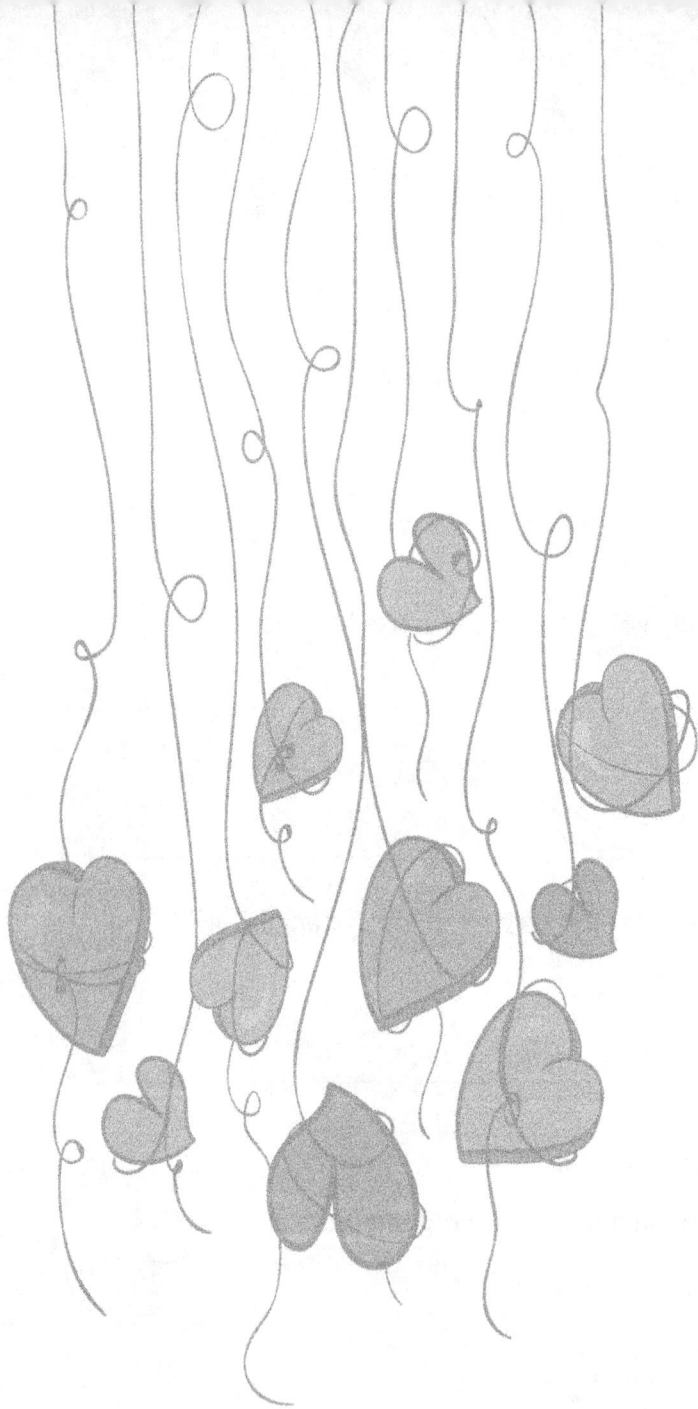

WEEK 27

Gonna Dress You Up in My Love

LAST WEEK, WE DISCUSSED PLAYING DRESS-UP DOLL FOR AN OUTING AND solidifying your place as the babe of your partner's dreams. This week, let's use what we learned on the receiving end to return the favor. Now that you've established a stronger trust in your relationship, build on that by switching roles in this experiment. As with any tip, this exercise will only work with your partner's freely given consent. If your partner is willing, for Week 27 of *52 Love*, let last week's dressee be the dressor.

We all wish for our lover to find us attractive. Last week's lesson taught us about the confidence connected with boldly wearing an outfit, knowing that your appearance appeals to your partner. Now that it's your turn to choose, search for items that highlight your partner's best attributes. Is there a blouse that flatters her figure? A skirt that hugs those hips you love to squeeze? Perhaps there's a scarf with the right splash of color to highlight the sparkle of her eyes. Use this opportunity to spotlight your partner's physical beauty.

Take care to avoid comments that diminish your partner's confidence. Focus on what you *do* like instead of perceived imperfections she may wish to hide. This isn't the time to suggest constricting slimwear for the sake of body shaming. Creating or feeding an insecurity complex will sabotage your efforts to grow closer. If you, however, go crazy at the sight of her favorite red corset cinching her waist, then by all means, ardently accentuate her assets.

The important thing is to make her feel loved and admired in the outfit you piece together. If she squirms from insecurity, bolster her confidence with the reasons you admire this look on her. If she grumbles about clashing items, work together to find something that satisfies the look you want while alleviating her concerns. As the initiator, you should accommodate her despite your efforts to avoid such conflict when roles were reversed. The onus is yours to keep the peace.

As you assemble her ensemble, help her into each piece. Glide your fingers along her waistband before you fasten the snap. Breathe in the scent of her hair while you pinch her zipper tab and slide it through its shiny teeth. Slowly button your way up the silky material that conceals her soft, smooth skin. Use the proximity as a means of foreplay, a promise of what's to come when you return home.

Once you hit the town, continue to assure your partner of her emphasized beauty. Smile when you catch her eye. Strut proudly beside her as you pass onlookers. Comment on how much she excites you. Pull a phrase or two from Week 9. And once you get home, show the same level of care as you applied selecting the night's ensemble when undressing your lovely lady.

Love Bites

1. Was this more challenging or less challenging for you than last week's intimacy tip?

_____

_____

_____

2. What are your favorite physical attributes on your partner?

_____

_____

_____

3. How do you like to see those attributes accentuated?

_____

_____

_____

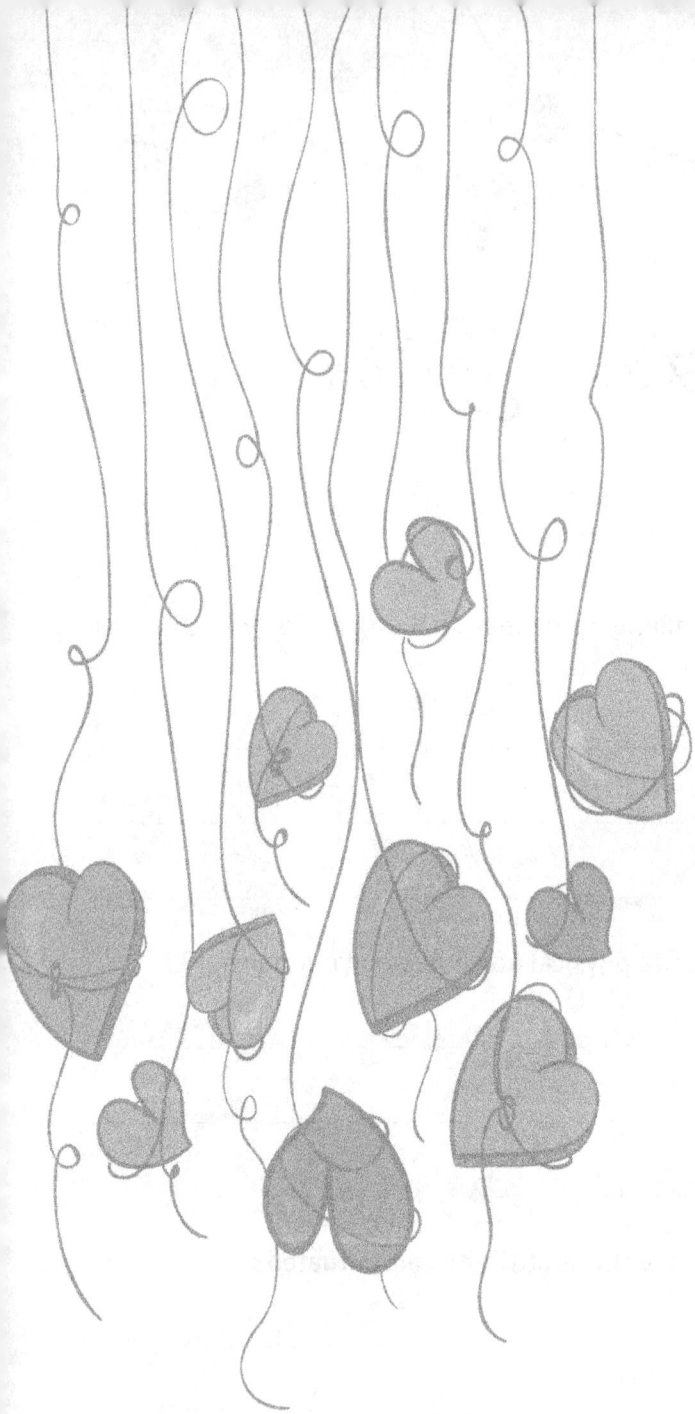

WEEK 28

Dress Up for a Night In

THIS WEEK, WE CONTINUE THE FASHION TREND. YOU'VE DRESSED EACH other. Now, it's time to dress yourselves—in style. Fancy clothes sometimes feel like an indulgence reserved for an outside cause. For Week 28 of *52 Love*, let that cause be each other. You and your partner will dress for a night on the town. Then stay home.

This week, as you prepare for a dinner date at home, let your personality shine through. Clothing and fashion choices are key parts of self-expression. In previous weeks, you've paid attention to your partner's wardrobe preferences. If your choices do not reflect those, perhaps part of your evening's conversation can include the motivations for your selections. For most, what we wear and how people react to it affect our self-esteem. Use this opportunity to reveal your vulnerability and deepen your intimacy. Encourage your partner to do the same.

Mood and clothing are intertwined. Dressing special will make you both *feel* special. Posture shows alertness. Alertness shows interest. Your posture improves when you dress well, which leads to a more attentive encounter with your partner. Even the ritual of preparing yourself for a night out will boost your spirits. Embrace the excitement of dressing up even though you plan to stay home.

Pay the usual attention to grooming as you would if you intended to leave the house. If you wear makeup, brush on a glamorous look. No matter where you use your razor, apply a fresh shave. Accessorize. Spritz cologne. Wear shoes. You can kick them off after dinner when you are in the relaxing phase of your evening, but to start your at-home date, complete your ensemble with a sexy boot or designer heel—whatever makes you feel most attractive.

Even if you keep the dinner simple or order takeout, dress up your surroundings as well. Tidy the applicable areas of your home. Light candles. Use cloth napkins. If you're a paper plate household, pull out the real dishes and flatware. Create an ambiance with the setting that suits your evening's agenda. As a bonus, open a favorite bottle of wine and enjoy to your heart's content.

The important thing is that you and your partner create an environment conducive to celebrating your love and demonstrating your importance to one another. Instead of making a statement to the world with your clothes, you're declaring your love for each other. *You are reason enough for me to look my best. You are what makes the occasion special.*

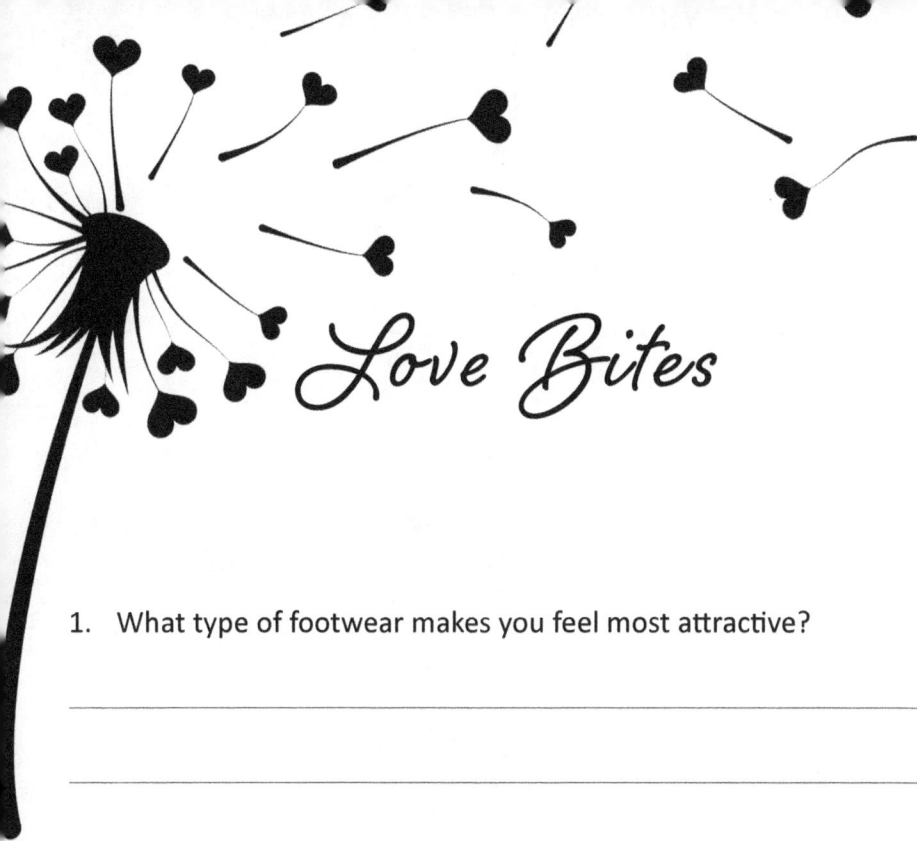

Love Bites

1. What type of footwear makes you feel most attractive?

_____

_____

_____

2. How do your clothes affect your self-esteem?

_____

_____

_____

3. How does dressing up for your partner differ from dressing up for a less intimate crowd?

_____

_____

_____

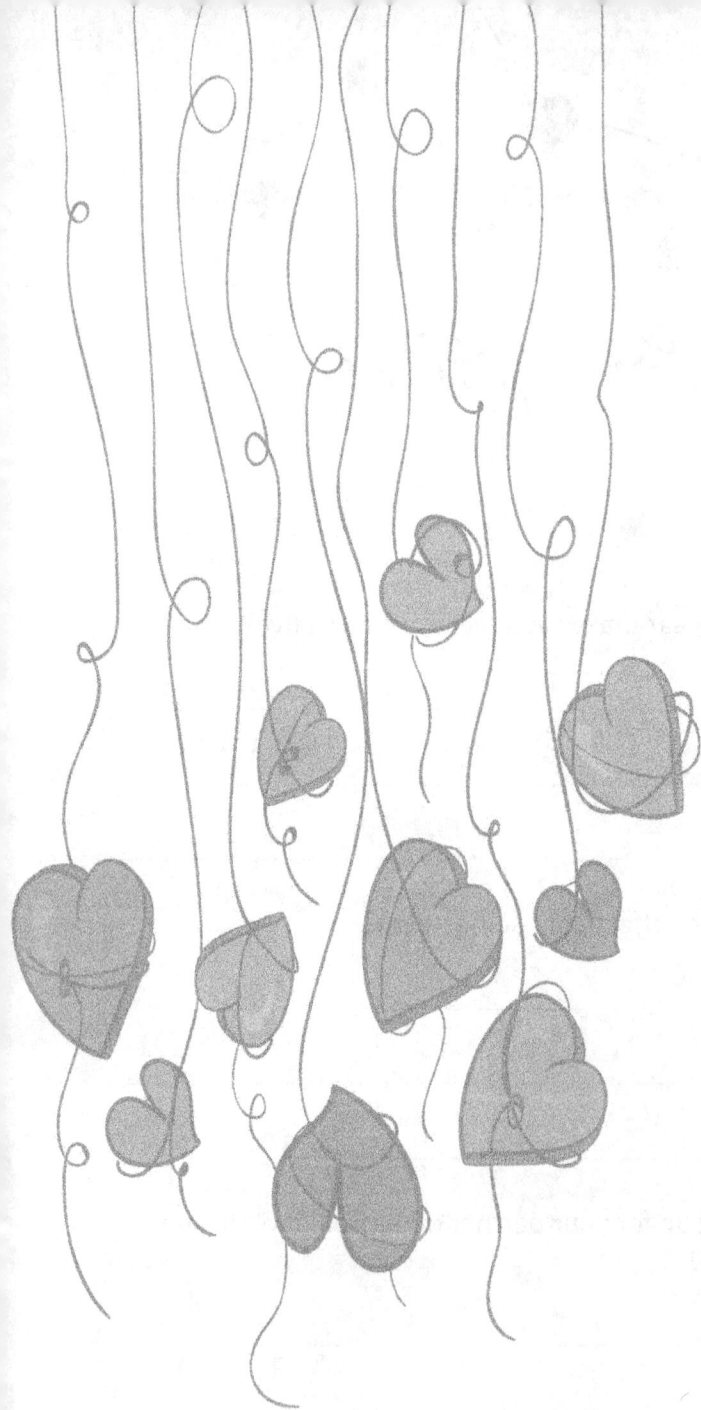

WEEK 29

Get out of Character to Get into Character

THIS WEEK, AS THE NEXT ATTIRE-THEMED INTIMACY TIP, LET'S STRETCH our imagination in a different direction. Many anticipate Halloween as a yearly excuse to transform, an opportunity to shed one's day-to-day appearance for something more exciting. Trying new things together keeps relationships fresh. For Week 29 of *52 Love,* transform your relationship by ditching your everyday costumes.

Cosplay can be as simple as dressing like beloved characters from a television series or as detailed as manifesting meticulous recreations of larger-than-life superheroes. Escape from everyday monotony by bringing your fantasies to life.

As a portmanteau of "costume" and "play," cosplay allows a fun way to reveal pieces of yourself that may usually stay hidden. Couples cosplay encourages you to explore those pieces together. You can dress as a fictional couple, share individual favorites with each other, or cater to each other's whims. Perhaps your partner has a character crush whose look really excites her. Imagine how she'll respond when she sees you dressed that way.

Some people want to jump right into character without the hassle of sewing and gluing pieces. Others love the thrill of developing the looks from scratch. Whether you and your partner choose to buy or create, embrace the chance to embark on a new adventure together.

If you're new to cosplay, no need to spend exorbitant amounts of money on costumes or props. You'll be surprised at the treasures you can find in thrift stores and clearance sections. If you and your partner have already dabbled in cosplay, maybe it's time to elevate your game with more elaborate costumes. Get creative with gender-bending versions. Or develop interpretations that you've always wanted to see.

One of you too shy to go all out? Wear something that doesn't attract more attention than you desire. The subtle suspenders from your Dr. Who getup may not garner the same recognition as full-blown Storm Trooper armor, but what the common observer misses becomes a shared secret between you and your partner. Rather than focus on outward dress alone, pay homage to the qualities you admire in the character. Sprinkle your conversation with phrases from your character's unique vocabulary.

Stepping into the boots of a powerful character can boost your confidence. Many cosplayers are shy, yet once they slip into their costumes, the character's traits shield the wearer from perceived vulnerabilities. This new strength can lead to playtime with your partner. Give yourselves permission to behave more boldly than you might ordinarily. Reinvent yourselves and your roles. Adjust your plans to your mutual level of comfort. Since you and your partner define the rules, there's no way to fail.

In time, you and your partner may extend your cosplay into bigger adventures. Throw a themed party. Hit the Renaissance Fair. Dress up for a children's charity. I'm not suggesting you sign up for the next cosplay convention, though if you and your partner are game, why not go for it? Whether it's for private enjoyment, public spectacle, or somewhere in between, revel in the new dimension cosplay can add to your relationship.

Love Bites

1. Which fictional characters wear the best costumes?

_____

_____

_____

2. If you could design your own costume, how would it look? What materials would you use?

_____

_____

_____

3. What costume would you love to see on your partner?

_____

_____

_____

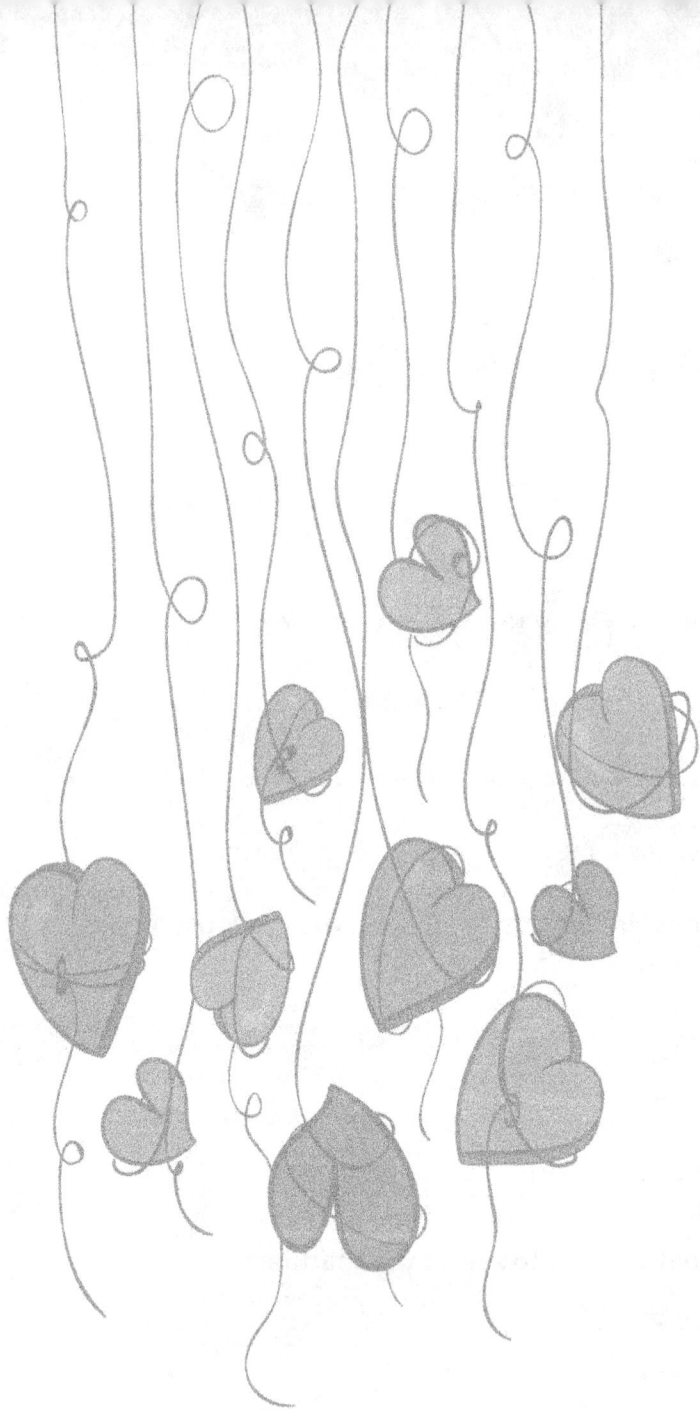

WEEK 30

Fulfilling Fantasies

WE'VE REACHED THE FINAL ATTIRE-THEMED INTIMACY TIP. ALTHOUGH
recent weeks focused on what to wear, this week may have your clothes
flying. For Week 30 of *52 Love*, engage in a seductive game of roleplay,
starring you and your partner.

Roleplaying can help overcome inhibitions. Some may fantasize
about dressing like a 1950s housewife while "the milkman" bends them
over the kitchen counter in broad daylight, a completely different experience than for contemporary lovers. Others may fancy the taboo of
sex with a stranger, regardless of the era. Whether you live a very con-
trolled life and secretly covet being told what to do, or you've always
wanted to tie your partner to the bed to please him a thousand new
ways, exploring your desires together will lead to a deeper, more intimate understanding of each other.

Fantasy intensifies the sexual experience. Playing through sexy scenarios as different characters allows you to embark through new territory together. Masked by your costumes, you can boldly experiment with dirty talk or different positions without fear. The uptight teacher will apply ruler lashings without hesitancy. Randy Repairman will embrace the naughty pipe puns that would make your usual self giggle. Let your creative juices flow as you invent your scenarios. And if you or your partner reach your limit, simply slip back into your own skin and voice it.

When approached from a partnership of sanctuary, roleplay strengthens the physical and emotional bond. However you initiate the topic, start from a place of encouragement. Assure your partner that the suggestion stems from a desire to grow closer, not from dissatisfaction with previous performances.

Fantasies vary. Roleplaying brings many connotations to mind. One person's French maid is another person's midnight intruder. Ignore what you think the world says you should want. Let go of unrealistic expectations that may discourage you from moving beyond your usual boundaries. This exercise is about realizing your fantasies and those of your partner. Those are the only opinions that matter.

Communication is key. The more you share, the better you can meet each other's desires. Ease into the conversation by asking about his turn-ons. Admit that the topic makes you nervous, too. Working through insecurities together will bolster against that vulnerability when sharing your fantasies.

Depending on your relationship, you may feel comfortable suggesting roleplay without reservations or perhaps you prefer an indirect approach. If the latter, consider watching a film with an erotic scene and asking your partner if he's ever wanted to try something like that. Be prepared to answer the same question. If the conversation goes well, you may be in the market for a sexy firefighter outfit, though whether it's for you or him, only the two of you need know.

Reading sexy stories to each other, or better yet, narrating original tales can open the door to sexual roleplay. These stories can help transition timid partners and pave the way to more elaborate playtime. The best way to get past embarrassment is through trying. If the character you're playing is free to speak, help your partner push through the initial bashfulness with sexy encouragements. And if you find your mouth too hindered with a gag or some other obstruction, then you're already well on your way to fulfilling fantasies.

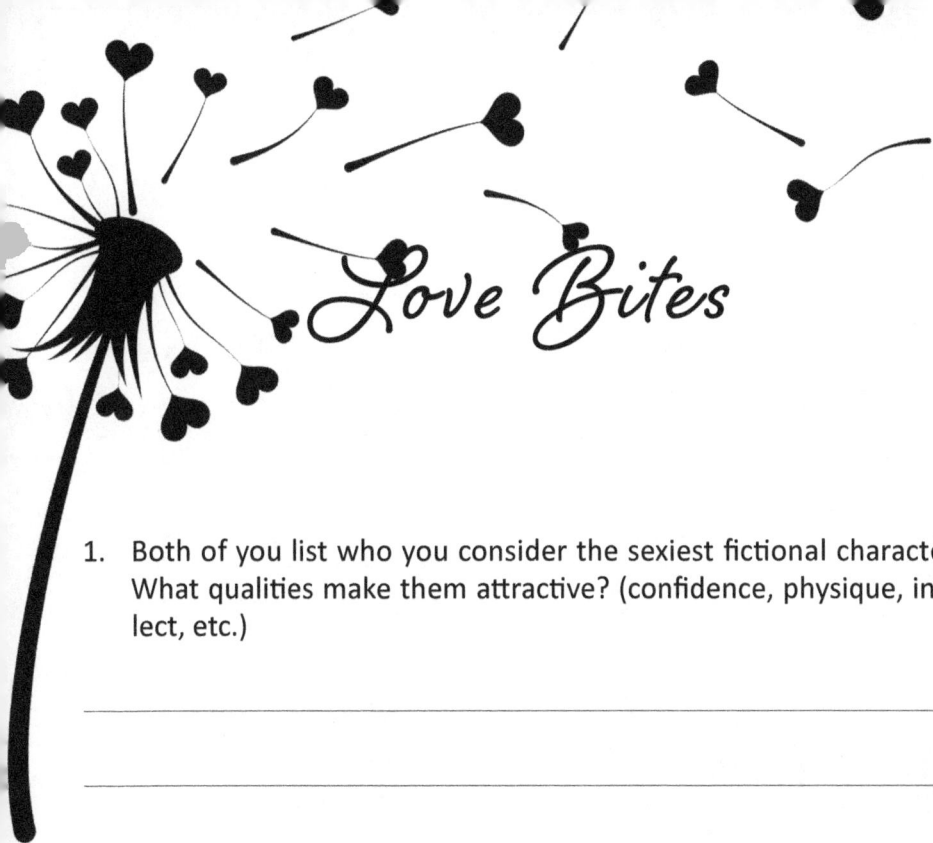

Love Bites

1. Both of you list who you consider the sexiest fictional characters. What qualities make them attractive? (confidence, physique, intellect, etc.)

_____

_____

_____

2. Do you prefer to make up new personas or to play as existing fictional characters?

_____

_____

_____

3. Hold hands and exchange secret fantasies you have not yet tried. How could you make those happen?

_____

_____

_____

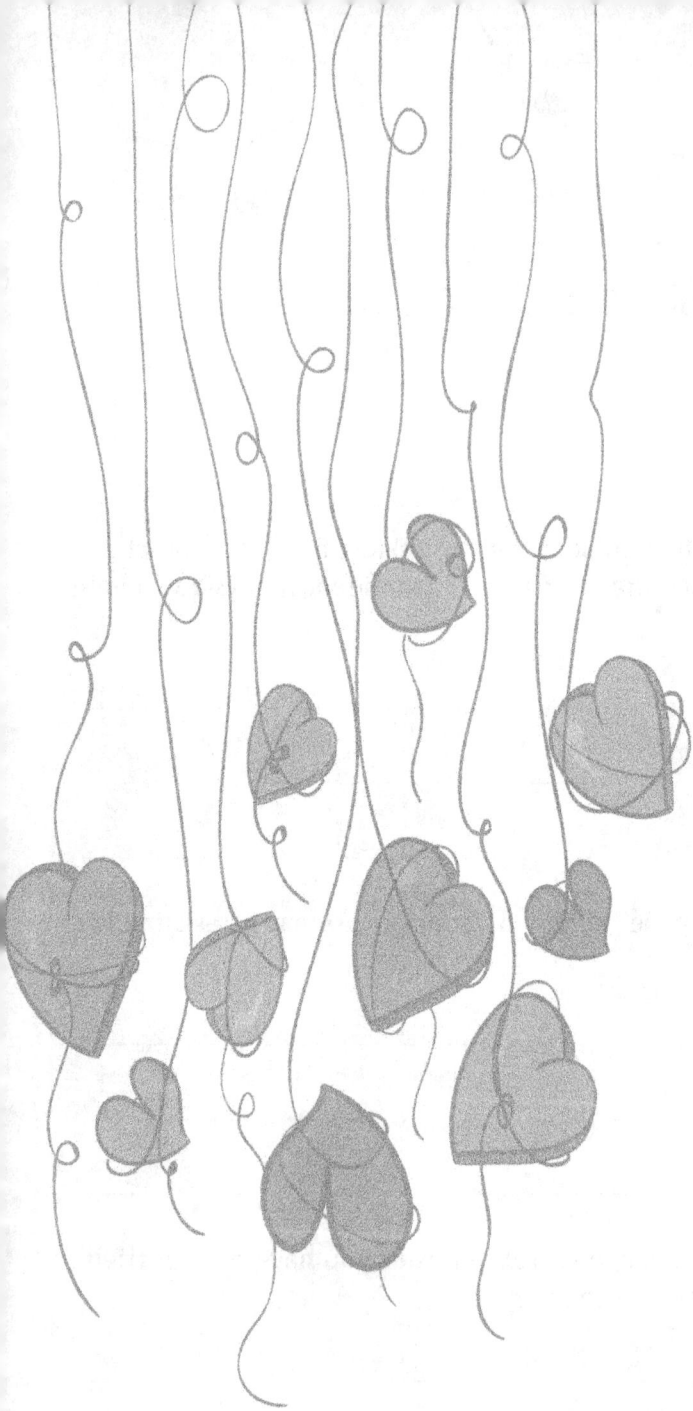

WEEK 31

The Joy of Nature

SLEEPING OUTDOORS ISN'T FOR EVERYBODY. I'LL ADMIT, IT'S NOT FOR ME.
My idea of romance comes closer to making eyes over a candlelit dinner. But I'm the type of author who listens to my characters. One charming scene-stealer has it in mind to take my heroine camping, despite her severe dislike for unhygienic surroundings. As he plotted options, his inner monologue swayed me into considering it as a suggestion for this series. As a bonus, I saw opportunities to practice earlier *52 Love* tips in new surroundings.

A camping trip helps you and your partner fall away from the outside world and live in the moment, be that an adventurous moment or one of peaceful stillness. As we've touched on in this series, our regular lives keep us distracted and busy. When you try to relax at home, it often feels like you should be doing something else—preparing for the future, planning another task, or performing responsibilities. Couples camping offers a chance to unwind together in a laid-back environment.

Escaping from home helps you disconnect from constant bids for your attention and reconnect with your partner. Let the natural calm ease your day-to-day tension. Hike an interesting trail, climb trees, bird watch in comfortable silence, skip rocks in a nearby pond. Use the break to unplug from digital life and enjoy each other's company, free from distractions and obligations.

Absorb the sounds and silence of nature. While strolling beside a riverbank hand in hand, enjoy meaningful conversations. Or don't talk at all. Quiet and solitude work wonders to cleanse your soul. Whether you're the type of couple to eat your daily stream catches or bring hobo dinners to cook over the campfire, prepping and cooking your meals together will serve as its own intimacy aid.

Outdoor adventures reinforce team mentality. Working together to set up camp—scouting a site, pitching a tent, preparing the fire— reminds couples they rely on each other for survival. Sitting across from each other in a restaurant doesn't do that. Without the distraction of other patrons or interrupting waiters, engage over fireside chats. Share stories—fun frightening fiction, cherished childhood memories, hopes for your future, or naughty tales to inspire the evening's climax.

And to that note, the great outdoors inspires primal urges. Being miles from civilization means there's no need to mute your enjoyment of one another. Screaming sexual appreciation is more fun than muffling cries of joy in the bedroom and even more satisfying than shouting your love from the rooftop. It's certainly more private.

Surrounded by the stillness in the air, slip into each other's arms and sink into the setting: a slight breeze, invisible crickets chirping, and the kindling crackling before you. Succumb to the draw of staring into a campfire together. Feed each other s'mores. Snuggle under the stars. Embrace the romance of quiet seclusion.

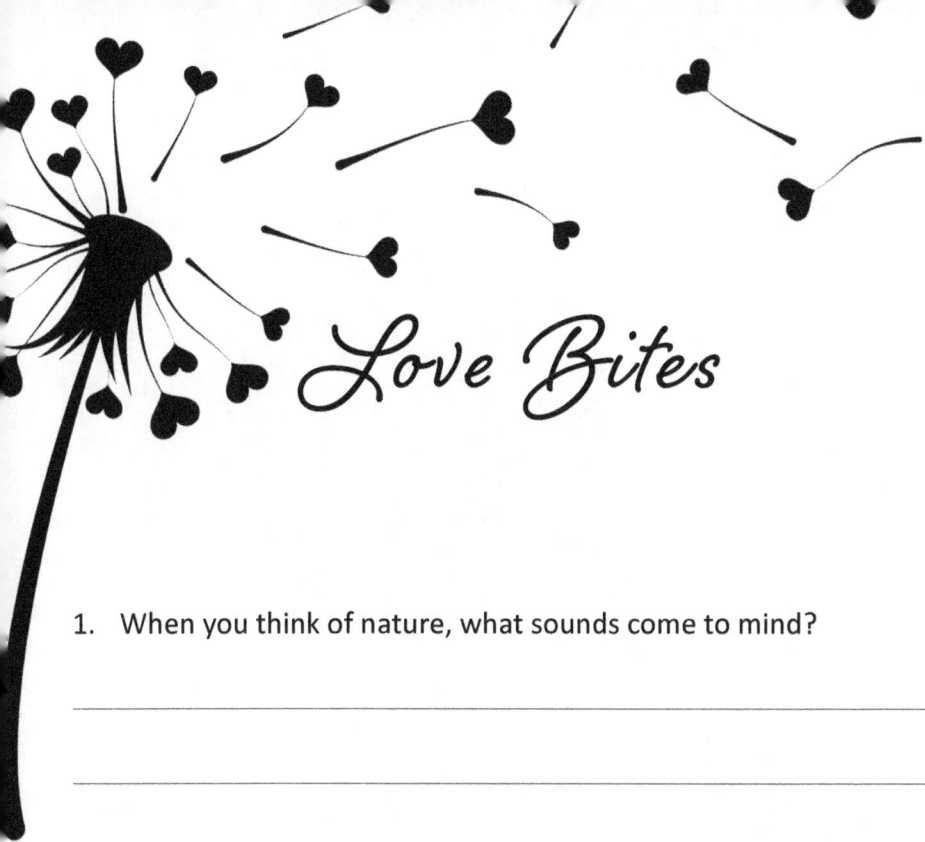

Love Bites

1. When you think of nature, what sounds come to mind?

_____

_____

_____

2. What are some of your favorite outdoor meals?

_____

_____

_____

3. How does making love outside differ from sex indoors?

_____

_____

_____

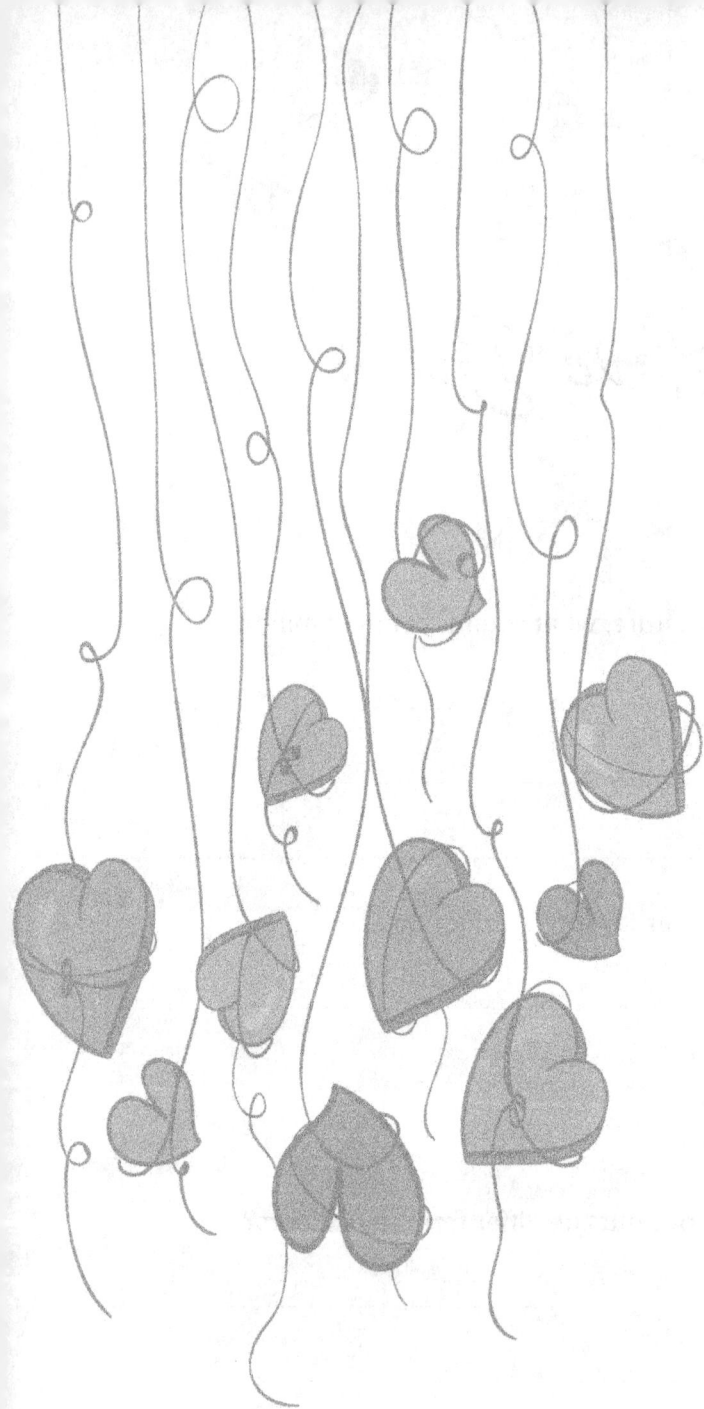

WEEK 32

Tour Your Town

WHEN PEOPLE HEAR "STAYCATION," THEY OFTEN ENVISION IN-HOUSE
entertainment. Let's expand that concept beyond the borders of
your home. I'm part of an organization that hosts an annual writer's
conference. A few years back, after a fun but exhausting day of learning,
a writer friend offered the faculty a personal tour of downtown Las
Vegas. It was a blast! I saw the city in new neon lights and learned
parts of my town's history I never would have known. That experience
inspired this week's post. For Week 32 of *52 Love*, take your partner
sightseeing in your own city.

Among the many benefits of playing tourist for a day, local sightseeing is a way to spend rich time together without spending all your
silver. Instead of paying for travel and housing, you can invest in fun:
tickets to that old haunted mansion (most of us have one) or burlesque

museum fees, or perhaps indulge in edible souvenirs. Or cut all costs, pack a cooler, and cruise the local arts' district.

You and your partner not sure where to go? Ask out-of-town family where they'd visit if offered a free weekend. Perhaps you have a well-informed local friend who can show you around as if you were new. Check websites that offer recommendations about what makes your town special.

View your city with fresh eyes and an open mind. It's easy to take a familiar setting for granted, but try digging into its history. Who is responsible for its origin and current state? What are the stories that bind it?

Rather than travel in the way you're accustomed, change your usual transportation. Walk a path you typically drive. Register for a tour bus. Take flight in a helicopter tour. By changing your method of moving through familiar surroundings, you and your partner may absorb the ambiance with an enhanced sense of setting and add a new dimension of appreciation for your home base.

When you tour your own town, old knowledge feels new again. Long-forgotten details resurface. Many annals update with the times. Embrace the chance to connect those historical lessons with the city you both know and renew your relationship along the way. Take photos to preserve the fresh memories from your new experiences with old places. Renew your love of the city and, with it, your love of each other.

Love Bites

1. What are your city's main attractions? Have you visited them?

_____

_____

_____

2. What are some of your town's secret treasures?

_____

_____

_____

3. Share something interesting about your city's history.

_____

_____

_____

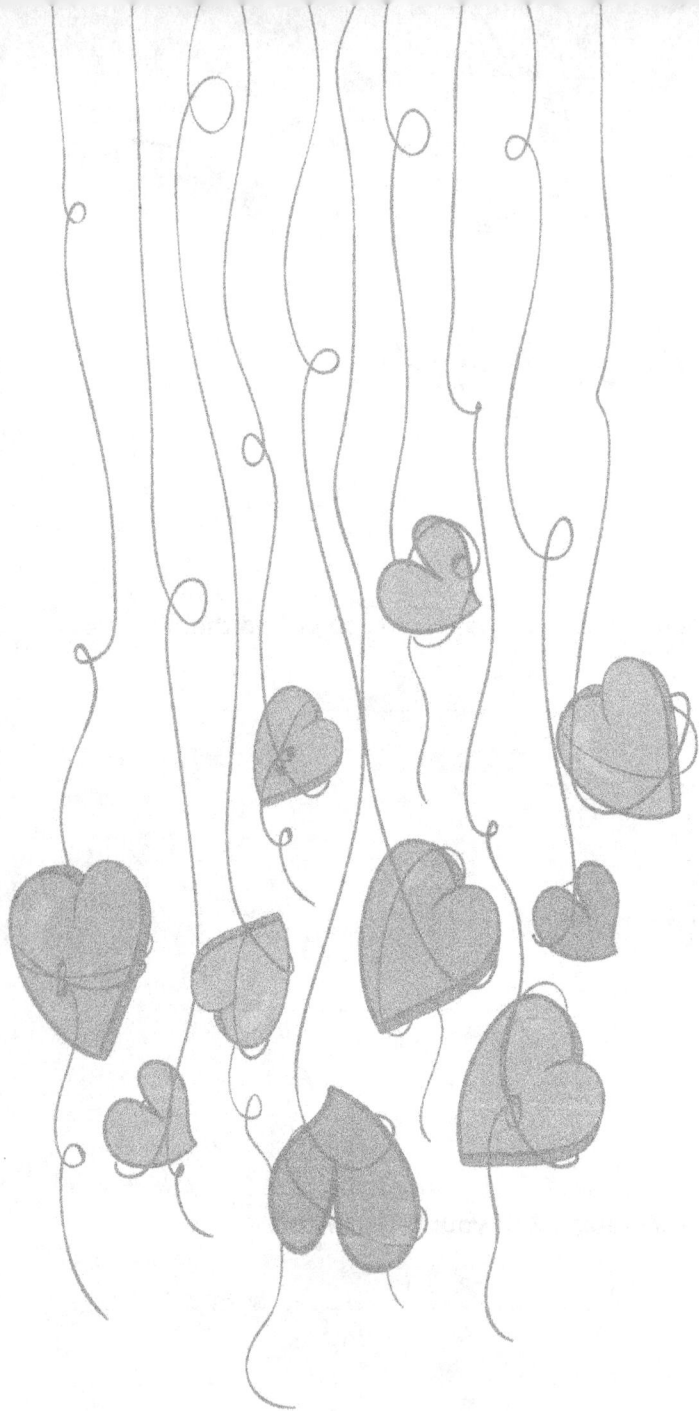

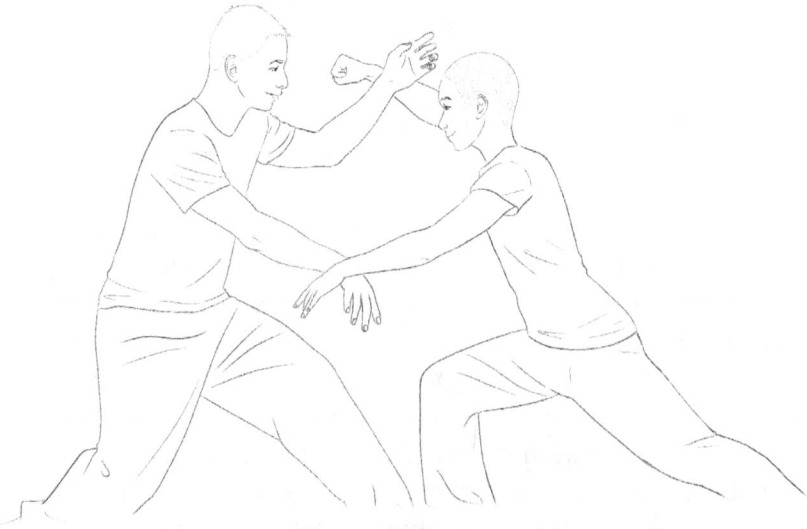

WEEK 33

Sweaty Sweethearts

❤

EXERCISE IS KEY TO MAINTAINING GOOD HEALTH. AND GOOD HEALTH IS attractive. Many studies show that working out with a partner keeps you accountable to your exercise regime. When that partner is *your* partner, it can also improve your romantic relationship. For Week 33 of *52 Love*, connect with your partner through shared physical activity.

Physical fitness benefits your health and wellbeing. Regular workouts with your partner build strong hearts and bodies while increasing your emotional bond. When the focus is on your own weight loss or fitness goals, inner demons can drown out the drive to improve. Exercising together supports each other's fitness goals, which often motivates more than solo ambitions.

The presence of a partner not only keeps you accountable to your exercise plan, it also boosts your performance. With a loved one watching, you're more inclined to push yourself. It may even spur competition. Let your partner's company galvanize you to improve while prodding her desire to work harder. Support each other's good health, and you will both reap the rewards.

Find an activity you both like or alternate your pursuits as a compromise. Be honest about what you enjoy, but be willing to try something new. This can be as simple as devoting more hours to light physical activity like walking, as organized as learning Taekwondo together, or as ambitious as tandem training for a 10k. Whether brisk walks, boxing, or boot camp classes, so long as you keep your lines of communication open, you are on the path to achieving your mutual goals.

Working out together will remind you and your partner of your initial affections. The effects of strenuous physical activity mirror those of falling in love. Elevated temperatures, racing hearts, and labored breaths are symptoms of sex and the infatuation stage of romantic bonding. Reignite those passions with your amorous muscle memories.

Invigorating activities stimulate dopamine and serotonin. These endorphins boost morale. Combine this physiological arousal with the increased energy and stamina from your regular workouts, and you have the perfect recipe for long-lasting intimacy. Rather than nose dive into a post-workout sundae, couples can devour each other. And dessert sex maintains more than good health.

Love Bites

1. How does having a workout partner help your physical goals?

_____

_____

_____

2. What are your favorite types of exercise?

_____

_____

_____

3. What is your favorite post-workout reward?

_____

_____

_____

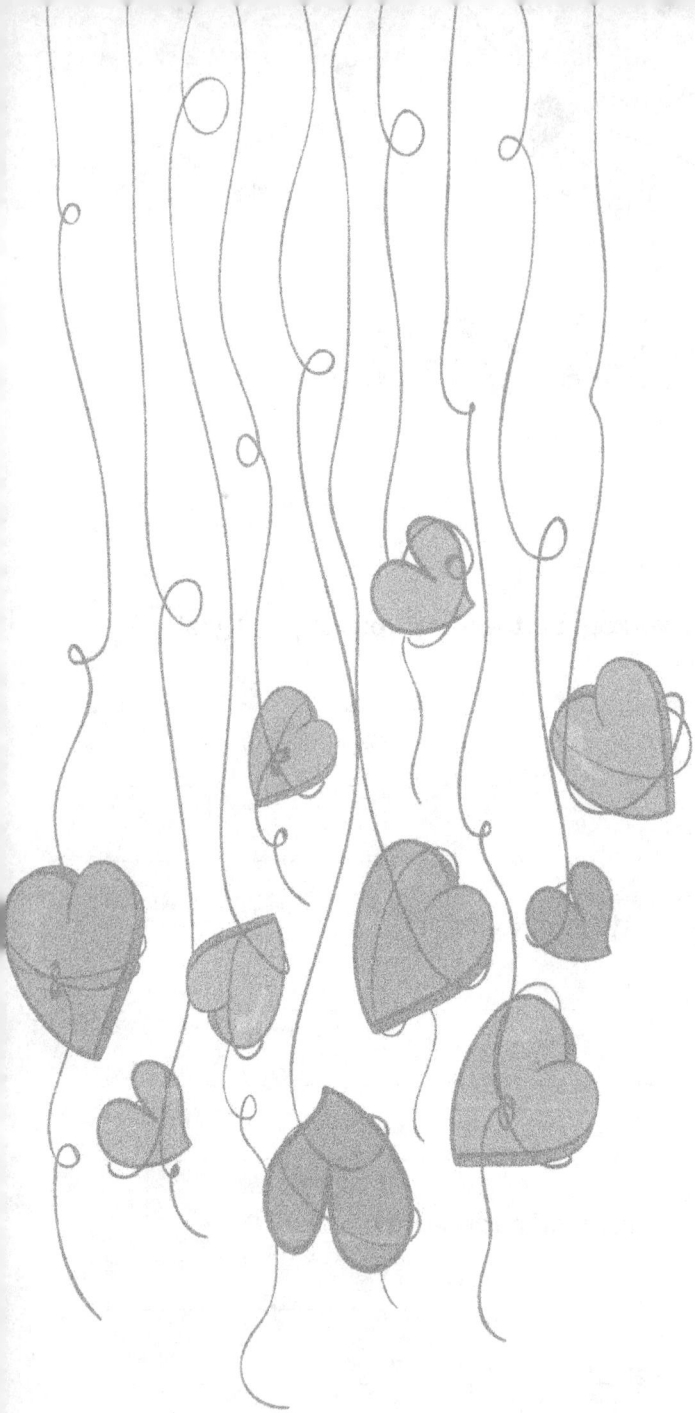

WEEK 34

Naughty Nooners

IMPULSIVE SEX IS HOT. AFTER THE INITIAL PASSIONS OF A NEW relationship fizzle, most couples fall into morning or evening lovemaking routines, a habit that can curb the libido. For Week 34 of *52 Love*, channel your spontaneous spirit with an afternoon delight.

Whether it's lazy weekend lovemaking or a lunch-hour devour-and-dash, afternoon sex can be the perfect way to rekindle your love life. Sex is a stress reliever. Afternoon sex helps you blow off midday steam. There's no anxiety about morning breath. And unlike in the evening, you're fully awake with enough energy to enjoy sex to its fullest.

Afternoon sex gives you the sense of getting away with something when you should be busy with responsibilities. It feels naughty, and dabbling in the taboo with your partner adds a hint of excitement. You can schedule an at-home lunch date together, then surprise your partner. Or wait for an opportune time and pounce on him. Even if you plan your tryst together, it feels spontaneous to toss aside usual daytime obligations for a quickie.

Experiment with outfits that don't need to be fully removed to reach climax. Think button-down shirts, spaghetti straps, or slinky skirts that slide up enough to grant access (this works surprisingly well for both genders). Practice Week 30's lesson by pretending you're having an affair. Take turns playing the sexy secretary.

The goal here is to have fun and enjoy each other. This experience should relieve stress, not create it. Keep the pressure where it should be—on your aroused nerve endings. If one of you doesn't climax during your first afternoon assignation, that's a wonderful reason to try again another day. Experiment with multiple ways to hit the high point. As with any worthwhile physical goal, frequent practice improves performance.

Make every minute count. Nooners are often quick, and if you're on a lunch break, you may need them to be. If you play them right, you'll have sex you can savor throughout the day. Start with a knee-buckling kiss before parting ways in the morning. Continue long-distance foreplay over text, phone calls, or email—just don't use the company channels! Let anticipation build during the morning so you are ready to tear off each other's clothes once you're finally within reach. When you return to your workday, resuming your torrid titillation with sexy messages about your rendezvous may lead to an evening encore. And there's nothing routine about that.

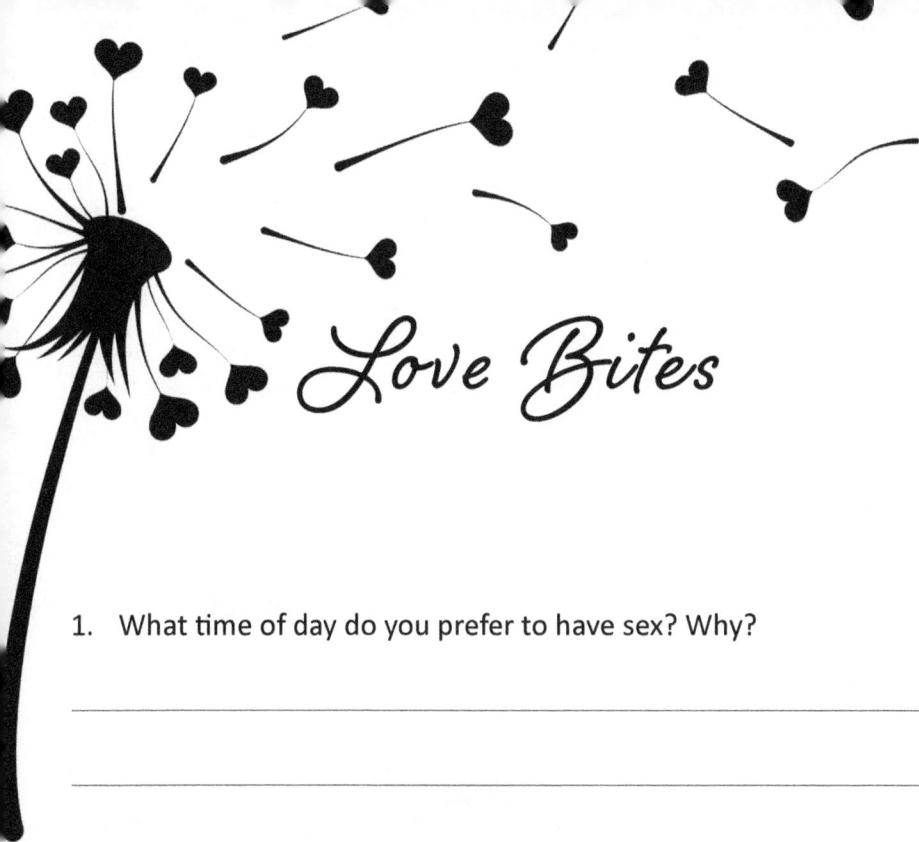

Love Bites

1. What time of day do you prefer to have sex? Why?

_____

_____

_____

2. Does sex give you an energizing boost, or do you need a nap afterward?

_____

_____

_____

3. If you knew you wouldn't get caught, what's the naughtiest place you would like to have afternoon sex?

_____

_____

_____

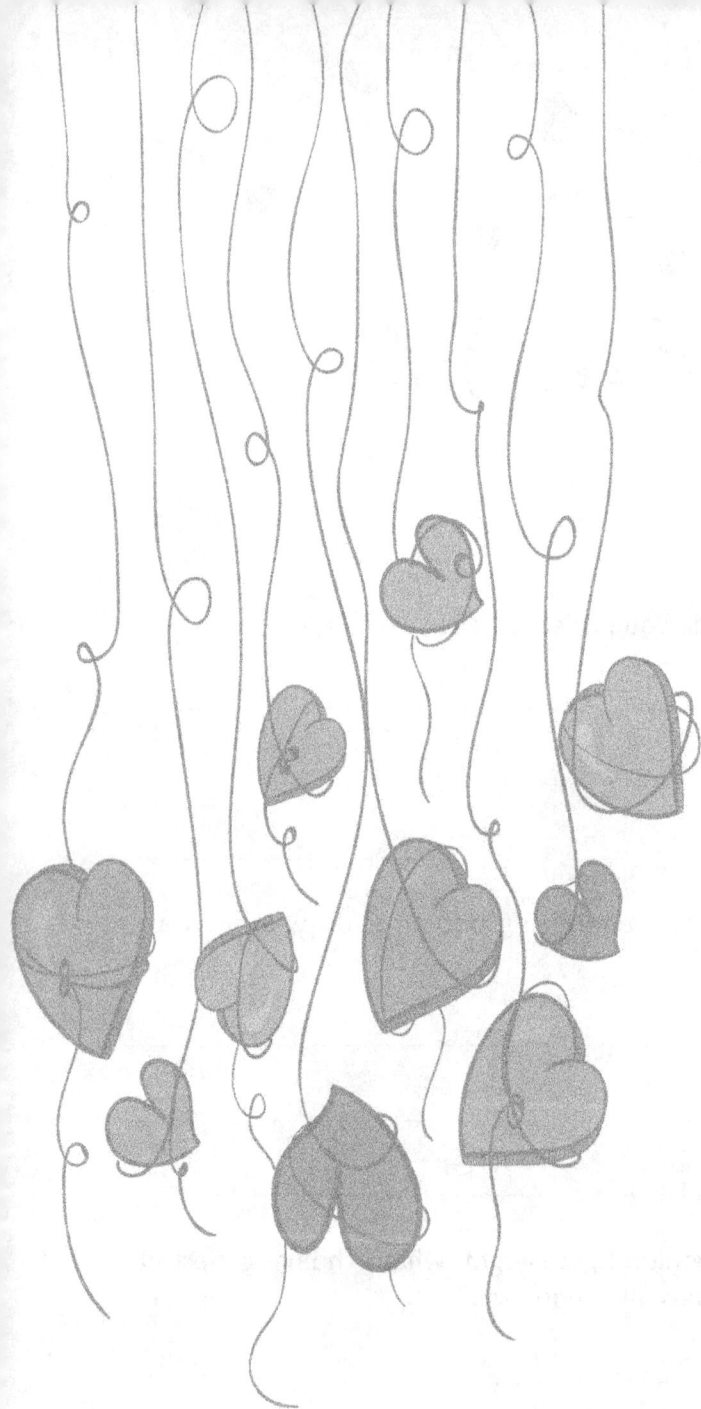

WEEK 35

Call of the Wild

ADVENTURE KEEPS LIFE EXCITING. THINK ABOUT HOW INCREDIBLE IT feels to enjoy a new thrill for the first time. Now think about sharing that joy with your partner. For Week 35 of *52 Love*, escape from the predictability of your routine lives and embark on an adventure together.

Exploring life as a couple means having a partner when you face challenges, overcome obstacles, and celebrate triumphs. Couples who seek adventure together push each other to reach unfamiliar heights. When you challenge yourself in new environments, you gain new perspectives—culturally, figuratively, and literally. Overcoming adventure-challenges together creates powerful bonds. Sharing joys from the high points strengthens those emotional ties.

For some, adventurous means bungee jumping from Macau Tower; for others, it's trying an untested restaurant. Whether you get your kicks skydiving, ordering the chef's choice, or something in between, sharing your wild escapades will bring you closer to your partner.

Many couples don't have the luxury of time or financial abundance to fly across the globe and backpack through Nepal or trek across Camino de Santiago. That's okay. There is plenty of fun available on a budget. So long as your adventure gives you a thrill that falls outside of your regular routines, it will spark excitement and bolster your bond.

Get lost together. Drive for an hour or two outside of your town and explore an unfamiliar city. For a wild twist, go undercover and assume new identities for your visit.

Explore the outdoors. Soak up some sun on a lake-boat rental. Paddle your way through a couples kayaking tour. Make memories while hiking a scenic trail. Climb a mountain and enjoy incredible views from the peak. Make a splash together snorkeling, deep-sea diving, whitewater rafting, or cliff jumping hand-in-hand.

Add a dose of excitement by doing something that scares you. Explore a haunted house, the kind that's open all year long. Test your teamwork in an Escape Room. Knock hang-gliding, ziplining, or a romantic hot air balloon ride off your bucket list.

Be children for a day. Go to the zoo, visit the circus, or compete in a game of laser tag. Relive your teens at an amusement park. Complete your circuit of carnival rides with a kiss at the top of the Ferris wheel.

Whatever you choose, your endeavor will reward with a gift you both enjoy three-fold: anticipation during planning, the real-time thrill, and savored memories to fuel your wanderlust for more couples adventures. In the end, it doesn't matter what you do or where you go; it's that you went together.

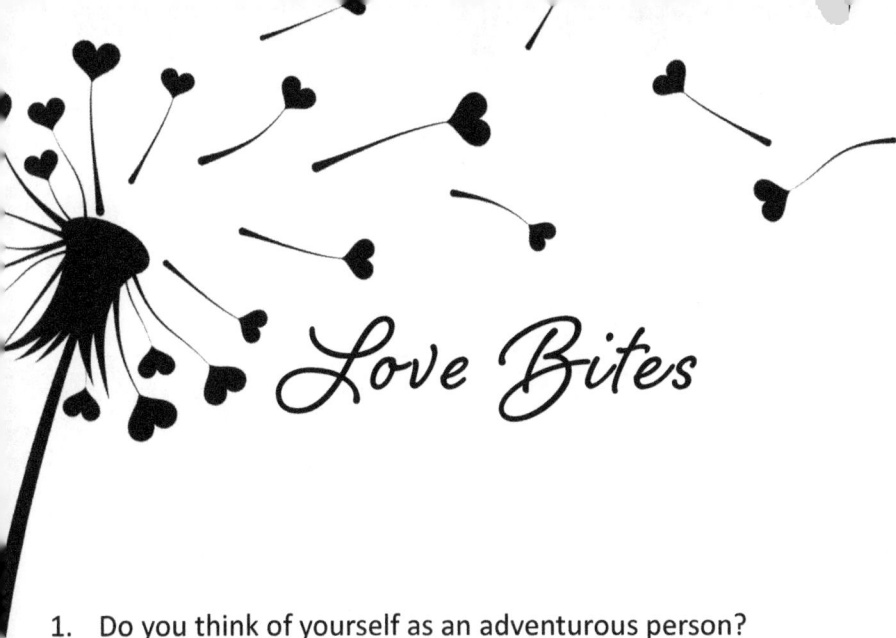

Love Bites

1. Do you think of yourself as an adventurous person?

_____

_____

_____

2. What's on your adventure bucket list?

_____

_____

_____

3. What could you do to make that adventure happen?

_____

_____

_____

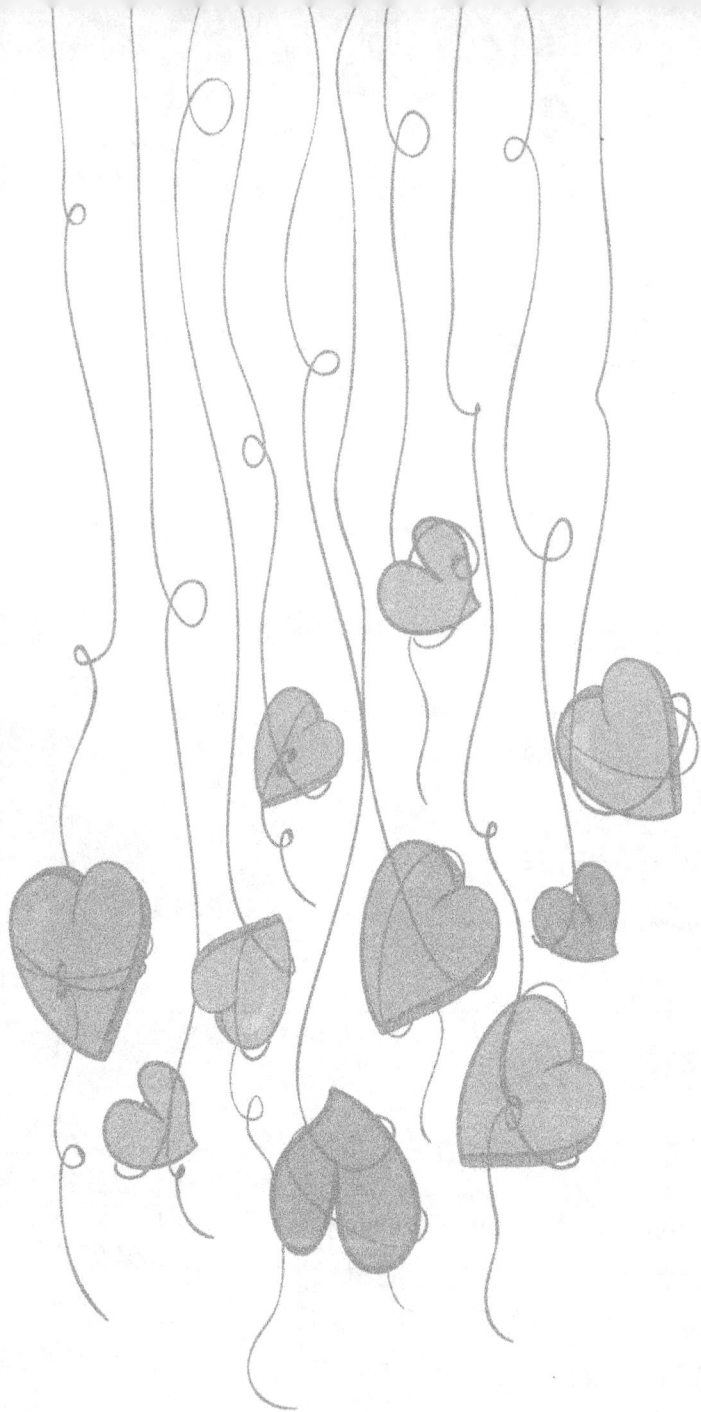

WEEK 36

Once More with Feeling

ANXIETY ABOUNDS DURING A FIRST DATE. YOU DON'T KNOW IF YOU'LL enjoy the food, the activities, or even each other. Yet hope blooms. You spend hours pining and preparing for what may lead to the greatest love of your life. For Week 36 of *52 Love*, relive the beginning of your journey with your partner and embrace the joyous anticipation of your first date together without the nervous jitters.

For some, your first date may have been fairly unremarkable. For others, it was an epic success, impossible to replicate. Try anyway. Let this exercise revive the excitement of your first date and remind you of its most memorable moments. Your first date marked the start of your relationship. Relish the memories without the awkwardness or uncertainty of a typical first date. In this case, you already know you're going to love the face sitting across from you (or better yet, beside you). There'll be no sweaty palms and no butterflies in the stomach. Just an exciting way to rekindle the flame, stimulate romantic urges, and celebrate the life you've created together.

Even if your first date wasn't wonderful, you can both laugh at the memories of what went wrong. And if your first date was truly terrible and you can't stand the thought of reliving it, either choose another memorable date to duplicate or recreate this date to reflect what you wish it had been.

Planning is key. You won't be able to replicate everything exactly. Try your best to recreate the feel of your first date with a few immersive details. Match the time of day to recreate the original atmosphere. Depending on how long it's been since your first date, you might be able to wear the same clothes. If you and your partner don't remember what you wore, try something from the same era or upgrade to the look you wish you'd sported. Preparing yourself physically will help you develop the right mindset for your second first date.

Recall the specifics. Did one of you bring flowers? Was this midway through a super-red lipstick or glitter eyeshadow phase? What music did you hear along the way? A playlist may be in order. If you moved from the city where your first date happened, find similar places for a comparable experience. The differences will feed conversation points. For an added bonus, call the restaurant where you ate and see if you can reserve the same table. You'd be surprised by the extents people go to in the name of love.

As circumstances allow, order the same food. Even if you *are* in the exact restaurant, it won't be the same. This is about creating nostalgia. Try to review the conversations you had, or pull out first date conversation starters. You might learn something new about your partner or answer a complex question you deferred at the time.

Put your best foot forward. This is a first date after all. Pull out chairs. Open doors. Use your best table manners. If your first date took place before smartphones were commonplace, leave your electronic devices at home. This will keep you focused on each other. Walk each other through your favorite moments from your first date. Which memories did you store as treasures? Spotlight emotional highs. Share the fears you squelched during your nervous moments. What did your partner do to alleviate them without knowing? How did this make you feel?

Keep the conversation on reliving memorable moments, sharing emotions, and getting-to-know-each-other questions. Resist the urge to discuss your current family, recent financial challenges, and present-day partnership woes. Instead, delve into each other's histories and hopes for the future.

Remember to flirt, perhaps more boldly than you did the first time around. Recreate the magic of the unknown by reminiscing about the flutters your partner inspired. Relive the anticipation leading up to your first kiss. Let that build up to what led to other firsts between you.

Depending on how your original first date ended, you can invite your date in for an encore or create a sequel that tops the original finale. And though you end your evening in the same bed, complete the reenactment by sending a goodnight text before falling asleep. Even if you are otherwise engaged before passing out for the night, it will be a lovely memento for the morning.

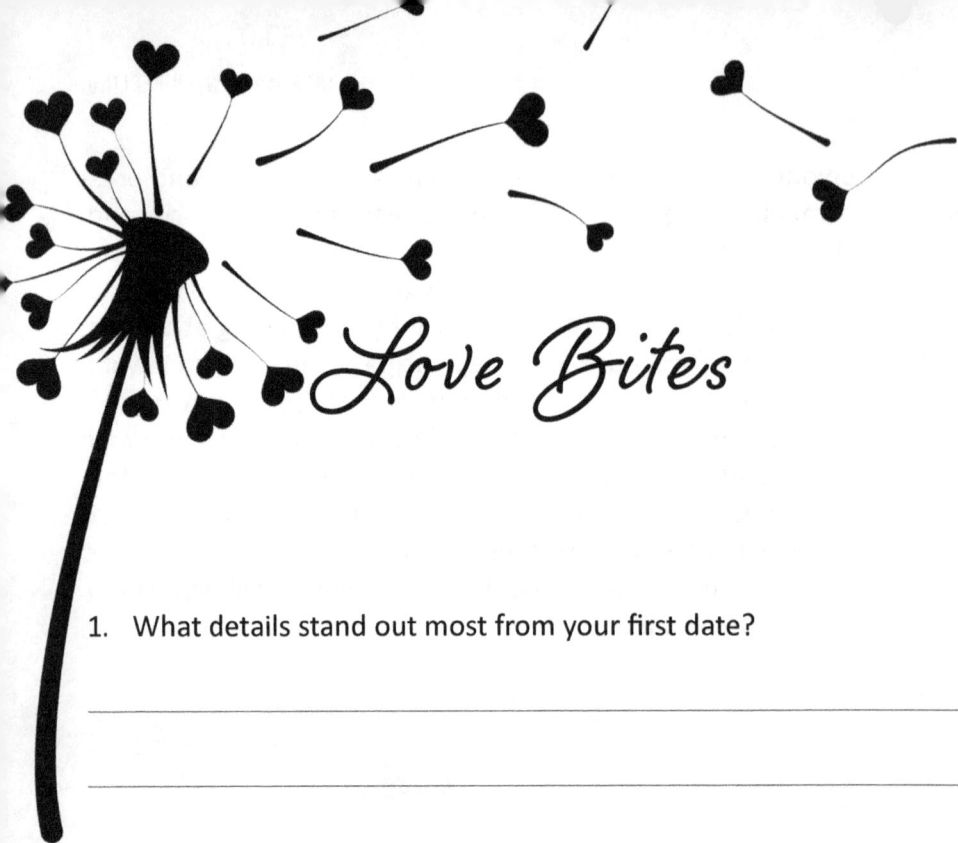

Love Bites

1. What details stand out most from your first date?

_____

_____

_____

2. What were your fears and anticipations before your first date?

_____

_____

_____

3. If you could go back and speak to yourself before that first date, what would you say?

_____

_____

_____

WEEK 37

Labor of Love

WE ALL HAVE CHORES WE DREAD. ANXIETY FROM UNFINISHED CHORES often creates relationship discord. At some point, most couples argue over domestic responsibilities. Whether both parties work at home, from home, or offsite, partners who assist each other with the household reap domestic harmony.

This week's tip won't debate the division of labor in your home. That's a topic for another book. *52 Love* is about helping you grow closer to your partner by actively working toward greater intimacy. In Week 11, we discussed speaking gratitude for the thankless tasks your partner regularly shoulders alone. This week, regardless of which of you bears the brunt of the household chores, show appreciation and humility to your partner by assisting with something she usually handles on her own.

There are countless tasks you could commandeer for your partner. Empty the litterbox. Take the dog for a walk. Drop off the library books.

Sweep the tile. Rake the leaves. Water the plants. Wash the windows—nobody wants to do that. The list is endless. And if you aren't sure how you can be of service, simply ask: "How may I help?"

If your partner is finicky about specific chores, such as how to properly load a dishwasher or the best way to organize the cupboards, you have two options. Steer clear of chores that might trigger a soapbox correction, or embrace your partner's idiosyncrasies and indulge her in her preferences. The former skirts a potential squabble. The latter goes the extra mile by communicating that her predilections are important to you. Either option serves your purpose.

Stress decreases libido. Willingness to serve is attractive in a mate. Higher sexual satisfaction is linked to partners who pull their weight around the house. Splitting the work means there's more energy for sex and more motivation for your partner to initiate it.

Your partner's chore list might be particularly long this week. Rather than grab for low-hanging fruit, divide and conquer the big tasks so you can regroup with quality time when the work is finished. Or reinforce that you're a team by doing the chores together.

Flirt while you work. Brush your side along hers as you wash and dry dishes together. Slip sexy banter into your conversation while you both fold laundry. Turn chore play into foreplay, which leads to the most intimate of post-work celebrations: messing up the sheets together.

Love Bites

1. Which chores do you prefer to do together?

_____

_____

_____

2. Which chores do you prefer to do on your own?

_____

_____

_____

3. If you could have your partner take over one of your chores for the next year, which one would you choose? Why?

_____

_____

_____

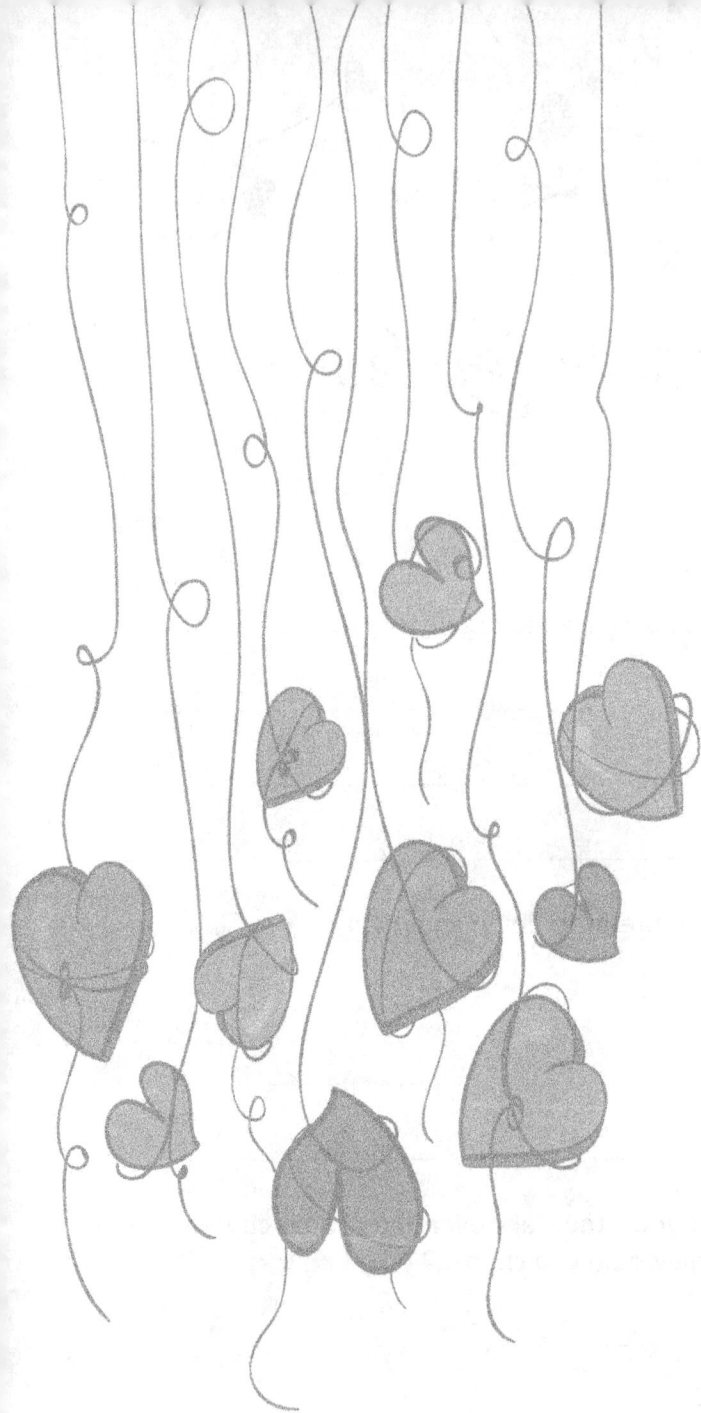

WEEK 38

Disconnect to Reconnect

WE'VE ALL EXPERIENCED THOSE MOMENTS. YOU'RE SHARING A BELOVED movie with your partner. The film approaches an exciting scene. In anticipation of your partner's reaction, you turn to watch his face. His eyes light up. His smile brightens. He chuckles and...

...it's all directed at his media feed.

No one enjoys getting phubbed—when someone ignores you for their phone. When your partner does it, the injury cuts deeper. For Week 38 of *52 Love*, unplug for some quality time together. Remove distracting phones, get cozy on the couch, and watch an uninterrupted movie.

Phone-free movie time might be a challenge for some. We've conditioned ourselves to have a cellphone within reach. Yet smartphone dependency has a negative impact on relationship satisfaction. Continual focus on your phone communicates that news apps, social media, and text messages are more important than your partner. Take a night to enjoy a movie together without the threat of interrupting pings, chimes, flashes, and buzzes.

Treat it like a first date. If during your introduction to one another you kept one eye glued to your phone, there probably wouldn't have been a second date. Not being available to everyone sends the message that your attention is valuable. Show your partner his importance to you by denying the outside world access.

Keep in mind, a cellphone's mere presence distracts your brain. Even when it's silenced. Even on airplane mode. *Even* if it's powered off. When your phone is within reach, some of your cognitive energy is tethered to it. Sever that tie by removing the phone from the equation.

To ensure the evening remains a no-phone movie night, leave your cell in another room, far out of reach for temptation. Focus on the film, breaking only to share a look or a laugh. Phoneless fingers free your digits for hand-holding or sneaky, snuggling strokes. And who knows? What starts with phoneless movies may develop into fully unplugged date nights. Enjoy dinner without checking your feeds. Finish a conversation without interruptive notifications. Revisit other *52 Love* tips. Go for a walk, read together, or complete a puzzle, all without phone distractions. In time, you may beat your nomophobia, improve your quality time, and make no-phone date nights a rule rather than an exception.

Love Bites

1. How challenging was it for you be away from your phone for this exercise? Was the challenge emotional or mental?

_____

_____

_____

2. If you could reclaim an hour of cell phone time per week for something else, how would you use it?

_____

_____

_____

3. Describe life before cell phones. Use your memory if you were there or your imagination if you weren't.

_____

_____

_____

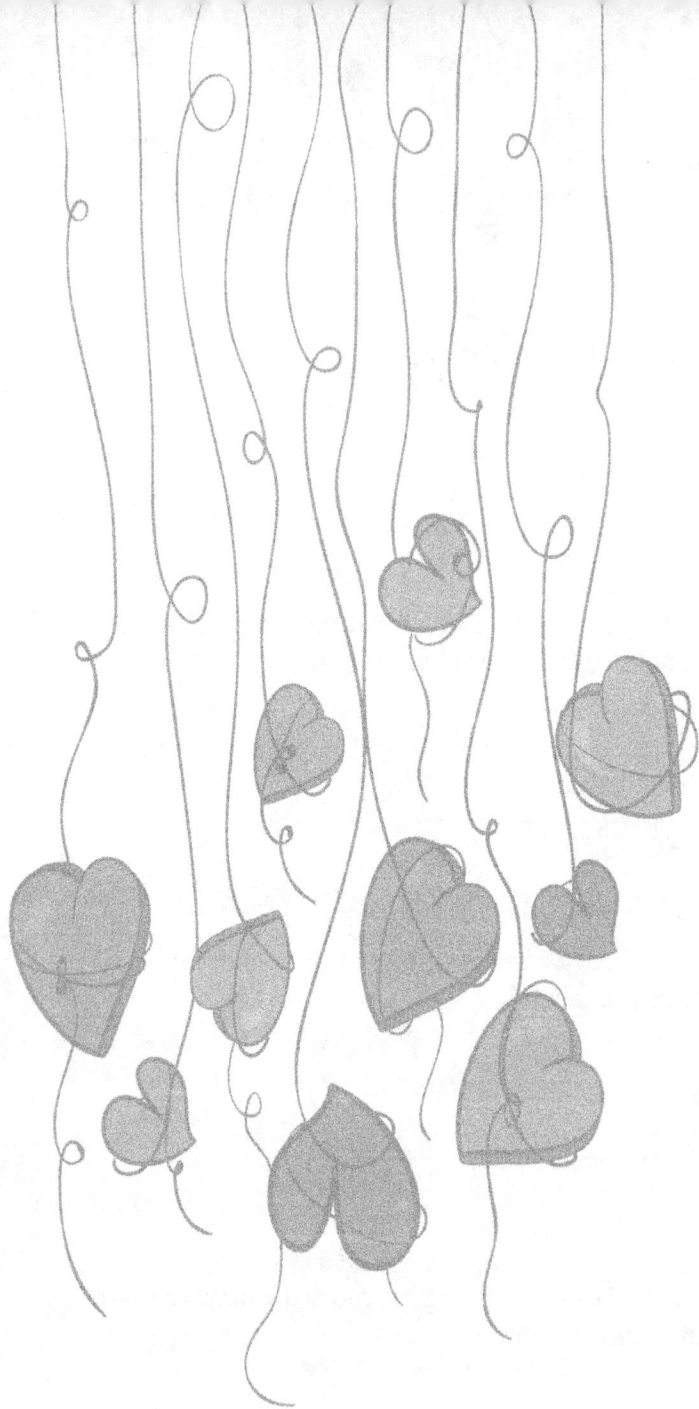

WEEK 39

Pique-Nique Mystique

❤

PICNICS ARE A DELICIOUS CHANGE OF PACE. COOLER EVENINGS NEAR early autumn make the perfect setting for outdoor eating. Whether you plan for day or night, eating alfresco allows you to change the scenery, escape the confines of your house, and experience nature. When you picnic in your backyard, you can enjoy the fresh air and open skies, all within reach of home comforts.

Though outdoor meals feel spontaneous, they require planning. First, check the weather. One benefit of picnicking in your backyard is that even if there are surprise showers, you're mere meters from shelter. That said, it's best to factor in the forecast to ensure picnic-perfect conditions.

Gather outdoor essentials so you don't have to make multiple trips into the house: napkins, utility lighter, bug spray, trash bag, maybe even an extension cord. Grab a box for an impromptu table. You can keep things simple with disposable plates and cutlery or take advantage of your proximity to home and use real dishes to add a dash of elegance.

Find a cozy nook with soft grass and a great view of the sky. Lay a comfy bedspread on the ground. If the yard is damp, protect your soft furnishings with a tarp beneath them. Arrange your blanket with plush pillows and a decorative duvet or two.

Hang rice paper balls, colorful bunting, or outdoor lanterns from low branches to boost the festive feel. Accent your setup with fresh flowers, votive candles, or battery-powered tea lights. Remember the picnic basket. Even though you're only a few steps from your kitchen, packing your meal in wicker will add to the ambiance.

Prepare a romantic playlist and connect to a portable speaker. Or if you've been together long enough to have a treasured mixtape from your courtship, go old school and dust off your antique boom box.

While it may be fun to whip up a gourmet meal to eat in a picnic setting, an easier option is to enhance the romance with finger foods you can feed to each other. Again, I fall to the example of my character Lucian, who whisked away his love interest for a sunset picnic, offered his lap as a pillow, read to her (swoon), and hand-fed plump, juicy grapes as an excuse to keep his fingers near her lovely lips. Imagine this scene between existing lovers.

Tantalize your partner with foreplay food choices. Butter-brushed baguette slices. Fresh strawberries and cream. Graham cracker cookies dipped in rich chocolate. Savory or sweet, accompany your delicacies with a bottle of wine served in plastic flutes (or glass if you trust yourselves with them in the yard).

Aim for minimal clean-up and maximum romance. Whether you opt for simple sandwiches or create a themed menu, the main ingredients in your backyard repast are you and your partner.

In between feeding each other delectables, indulge in your private setting. Hidden in your backyard, hands are free to roam without concern of public detection. Wear loose clothing for easier access. Slip your fingers between cotton and skin as a precursor to your indoor fun. Bon appétit!

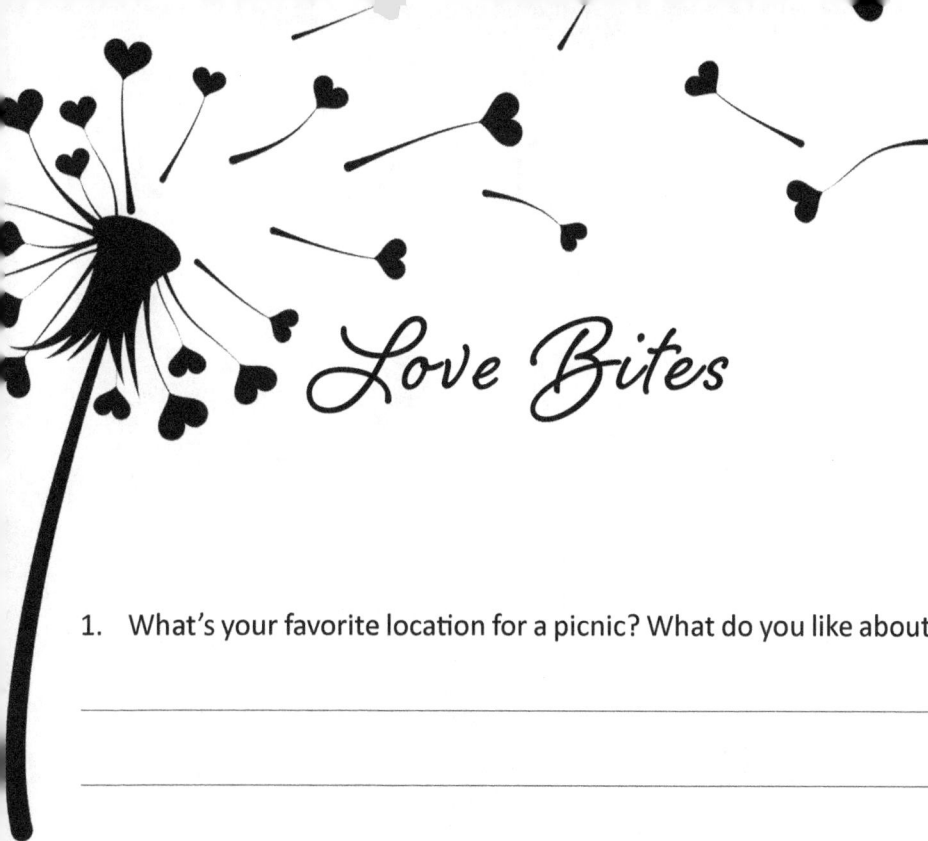

Love Bites

1. What's your favorite location for a picnic? What do you like about it?

_____

_____

_____

2. What are some of your favorite picnic foods?

_____

_____

_____

3. What's your favorite time of day for a picnic? Morning? Midday? Sunset? Midnight? Something else? Why?

_____

_____

_____

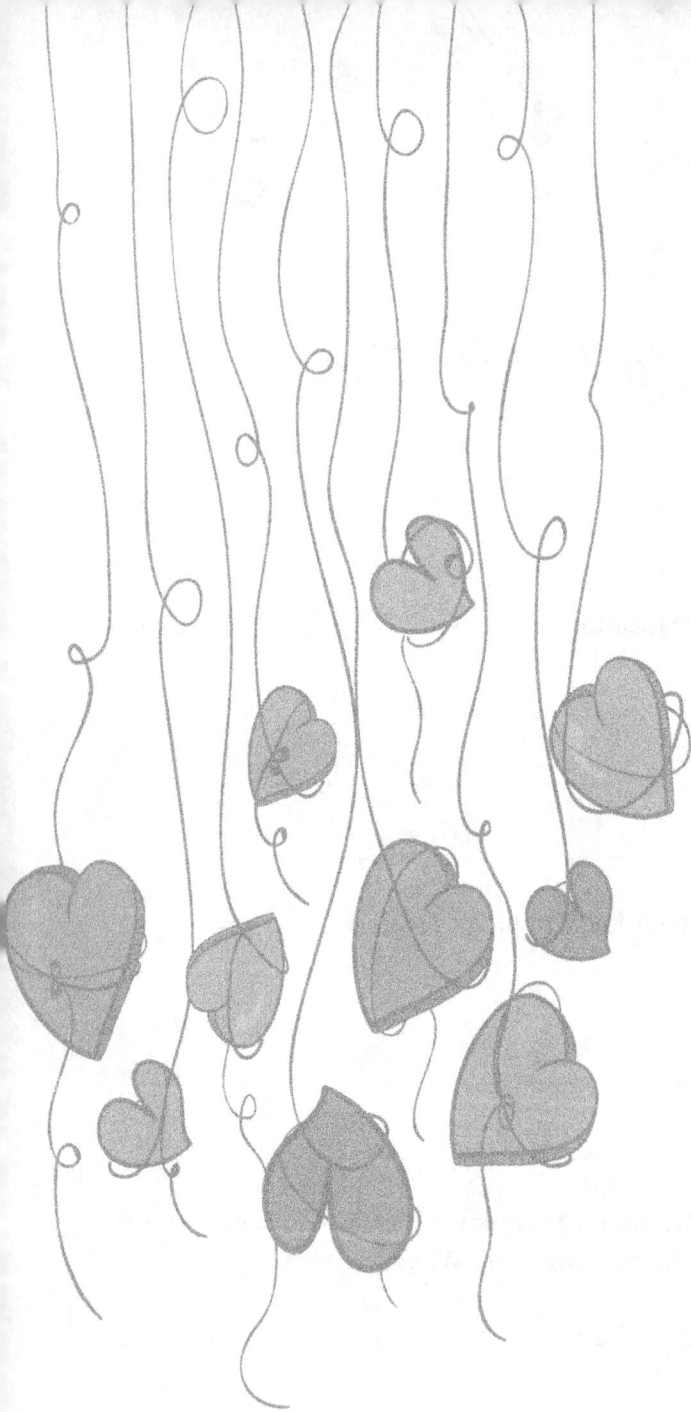

WEEK 40

Paint by Lovers

PAINTING CAN BE AS MESSY AS IT IS FUN. ON ITS OWN, PAINTING IS A stress-relieving hobby. When painting with your partner, your activity morphs into quality time full of laughter, conversation, playful banter, and shared creativity. For Week 40 of *52 Love*, treat your love as a work of art.

Consider your options for how you'll create together. Share a canvas: you and your partner work together, dipping into paint, blending colors, and brushing strokes toward a single collaborative goal. Or design a tandem diptych: place separate canvases side by side. You and your partner paint half a single picture on your respective canvases. When joined, they create one image. Like you and your partner, the two become one.

Collect your materials before cracking open your acrylics: canvas(es), easel(s), brushes, aprons, palette (even a paper plate will do), and of course, a variety of colorful paints. Purchase completed kits online or shop hobby stores that offer budget-priced supplies.

Acrylic washes off skin but stains clothing. Wear something appropriate, or if you don't wish to risk your apparel, decorate your canvas au naturel. Depending on how wild you plan to get, a tarp may be in order.

Allow at least two hours. You can't rush great art. See where your creative juices take you. Stroke your canvas at a slow and steady pace. Score your affair with music to set the mood. Pour your favorite libations. Keep snacks on hand to keep up your energy. Then ease into an experience teeming with romance and relaxation.

There's no pressure to paint the next Picasso. Choose simple designs that please your eye. Take a familiar image and alter the colors. Enlist the help of an online step-by-step tutorial. Or let your imaginations run wild as your collective passions splash the canvas. No matter your (or your partner's) level of artistic skill, your painting will make a lovely memento you both can treasure forever, almost as much as you do each other.

Love Bites

1. What kind of art do you like most—paintings, sculpture, ceramics, etc.?

_____

_____

_____

2. In general, does your opinion about artwork change the longer you look at it?

_____

_____

_____

3. Which paint colors speak to you most? What do they say?

_____

_____

_____

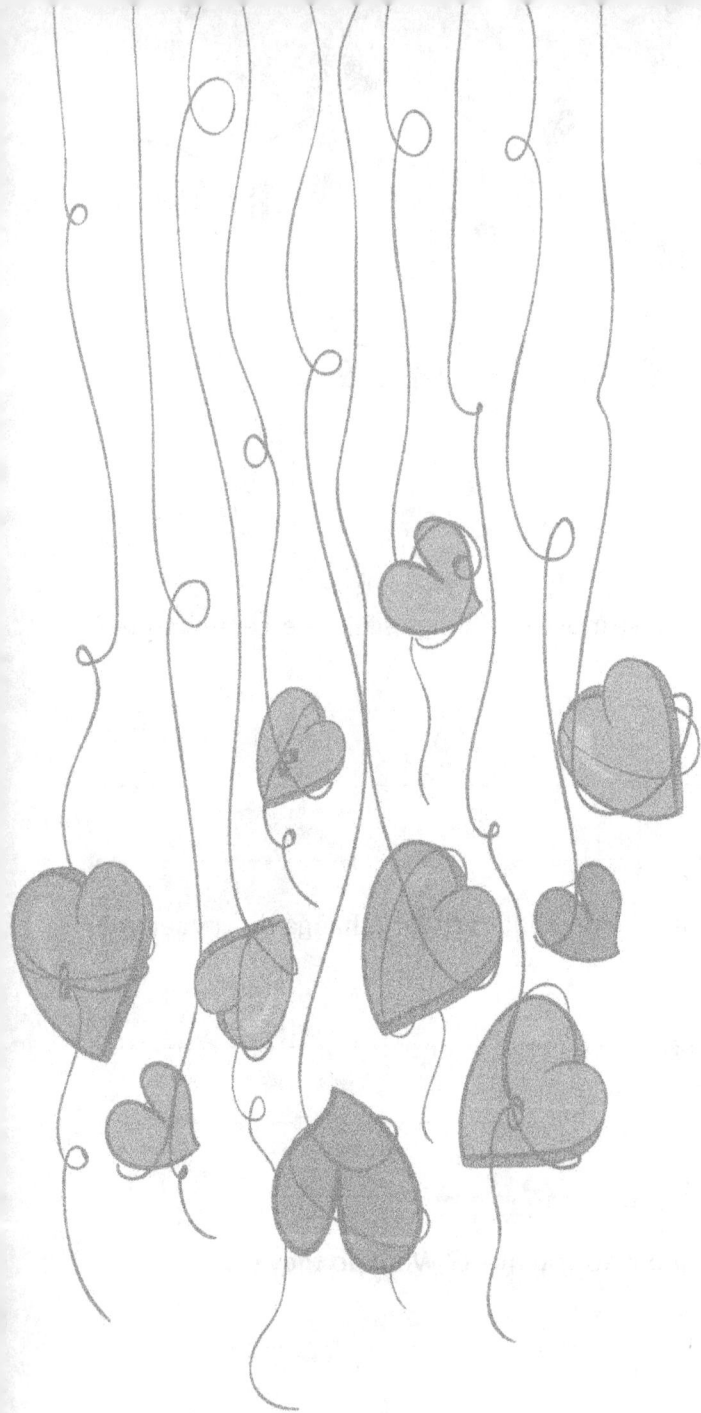

WEEK 41

Lip Service

WHEN IT COMES TO ROMANCE, SHAKESPEARE HAS THE BEST WAY WITH words. Rather than ask for a kiss directly, his Romeo wooed Juliet by suggesting they "let lips do what hands do." Whether you are looking to form sensuous habits to fuel your passion for decades, or you need a way to reignite those passions, use this week to follow the Bard's advice.

Pre-relationship kisses spark emotional fireworks and set your stomach aflutter. Once you establish yourselves as a couple, the frequency of those liplocks might dwindle. The chaos and stress of everyday life can overwhelm the most committed couples. When life pulls you in several different directions, use kissing to bring you back together and keep you centered on each other.

Regular kissing fosters security. Even a quick peck in greeting or parting restores your connection. It reminds your partner that whatever challenges the day brings, she is not alone. Think of your kisses as the glue that holds your partnership together. When words fail, you can still communicate your heart with your lips. Kisses are such a universal communicator of love that mammals who can't speak our language use them to share their affection. In this way, use your lips to fortify your relationship against the world's stressors.

Kisses create emotional intimacy. Through physical contact, you and your partner share your vulnerability in the comfort of each other's space. Being so close physically lowers emotional barriers and builds a foundation of trust.

Habitual kissing can also produce hormones that decrease stress and calm your neural system. Dopamine release gives pleasure. Oxytocin promotes bonding. Kissing triggers both. Even if you are anxious before you kiss, the act itself soothes anxiety. Once your lips touch, your focus is on each other and the intense sensations your kiss sparks.

The combination of decreased stress and increased pleasure boosts your immune system. That's right; kissing is good for your health! Unlike exercise or nutrition, which need time to take effect, the benefits of kissing are immediate. If one good kiss can affect you this much, imagine what a night of snogging can do.

Kissing is natural foreplay, but it doesn't have to provoke more. When you practice this week's lesson, treat the kiss itself as a sexual act. Lead into it. Take it slow to build excitement. Nuzzle noses. Mingle breaths. Brush your lips along hers. Tease with your tongue.

Go in for the kiss. Then back away. Make her *want* before you sate her craving. Then crash your mouths together in a mash of longing, lust, and love. Inhale her scent. Taste her tongue. Feel the passionate press of her lips. Then practice your kisses on other areas of her body. Let every part of your partner feel the depth of your love. When you're through, you'll ensure that those butterflies from your early days keep their wings.

Love Bites

1. Are you comfortable kissing in public, or do you need privacy to enjoy it?

_____

_____

_____

2. What are your favorite body parts for your partner to kiss?

_____

_____

_____

3. Describe the sensations when your partner kisses you there.

_____

_____

_____

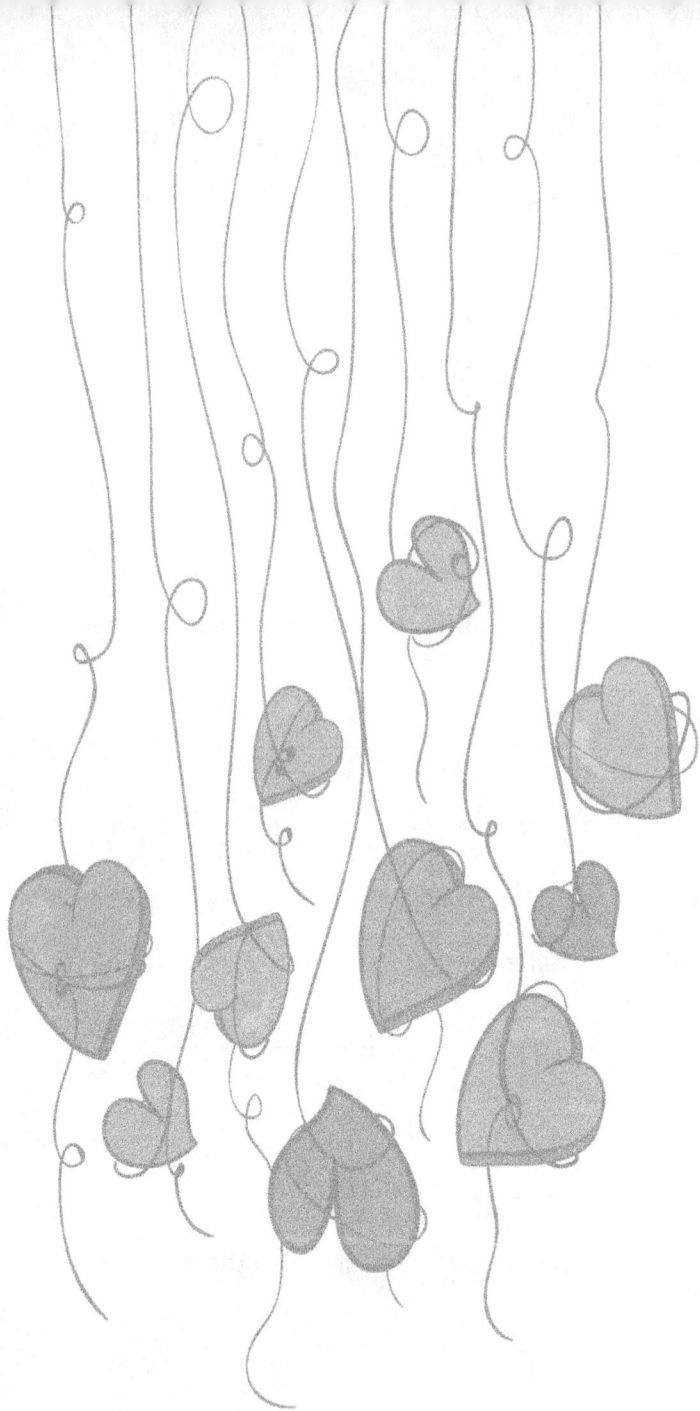

WEEK 42

Keep Him Guessing

❤

FALLING INTO A COMFORTABLE ROUTINE WITH YOUR PARTNER IS ONE mark of a successful relationship. And though routines help smooth everyday activities, they don't promote romance or passion. Even the most dynamic couples have their mundane moments. Surprises spark thrills, wonder, and a burst of elation. For Week 42 of *52 Love*, answer "the ultimate question of life, the universe, and everything" by stimulating unexpected joy.

One reason birthdays and gift-giving holidays are so exciting is the element of surprise those presents bring. Anticipation surges between both parties during the exchange. As the receiver sheds the package, revealing the gift, the giver watches for his reaction with similar hopeful expectation. When successful, the shared jolt of joy enhances their bond. Both sets of eyes brighten, and they share a look of love and gratitude.

A surprise can be as simple as buying flowers for no reason or as extravagant as planning a weekend getaway. So long as it triggers unexpected *Happy*, you have accomplished your goal. The intent behind your surprise is the intimate moment you create. The residual reward is the shared memory of that moment.

Choose an ordinary day for your surprise. Without the expectation of a gift, the delight doubles. As does the appreciation. Focus on your partner's desires, not yours, even if it means going outside your comfort zone. Unexpected tickets to see the Dodgers might excite you, but if it's not your partner's ball game, find another way to knock it out of the park.

Over the course of *52 Love*, we've covered many tips that could serve this purpose. Talk dirty for a night. Relive your first date. Tackle your partner's to-do list. Treat him to an unplanned afternoon delight. Or spring a new pleasure on your partner, a unique gift specific to him. Cue up a movie he's been begging you to watch, then sit through it with the aim to enjoy. Tell him he looks nice before he asks. Prepare a treasure hunt around your house. Nibble his sweet spot on the sly when you're in public. Leave a naughty note for him to find when you're apart.

Feeling ambitious? Create the ultimate surprise by masterminding an experience from his bucket list. Take one of those intimate goals or secret fantasies he shared with you in your couples journal and make it a reality. Amaze your partner by demonstrating your attention to his dreams.

Sprinkling unpredictable moments into your life with your partner can add a spark of delight that keeps your routine days vibrant. When you look back on your years together, you'll find a journey full of surprises.

Love Bites

1. Describe your physical response to receiving a surprise.

_____

_____

_____

2. Which do you enjoy more: giving or receiving surprises?

_____

_____

_____

3. Share a surprise that you didn't know you wanted until you received it.

_____

_____

_____

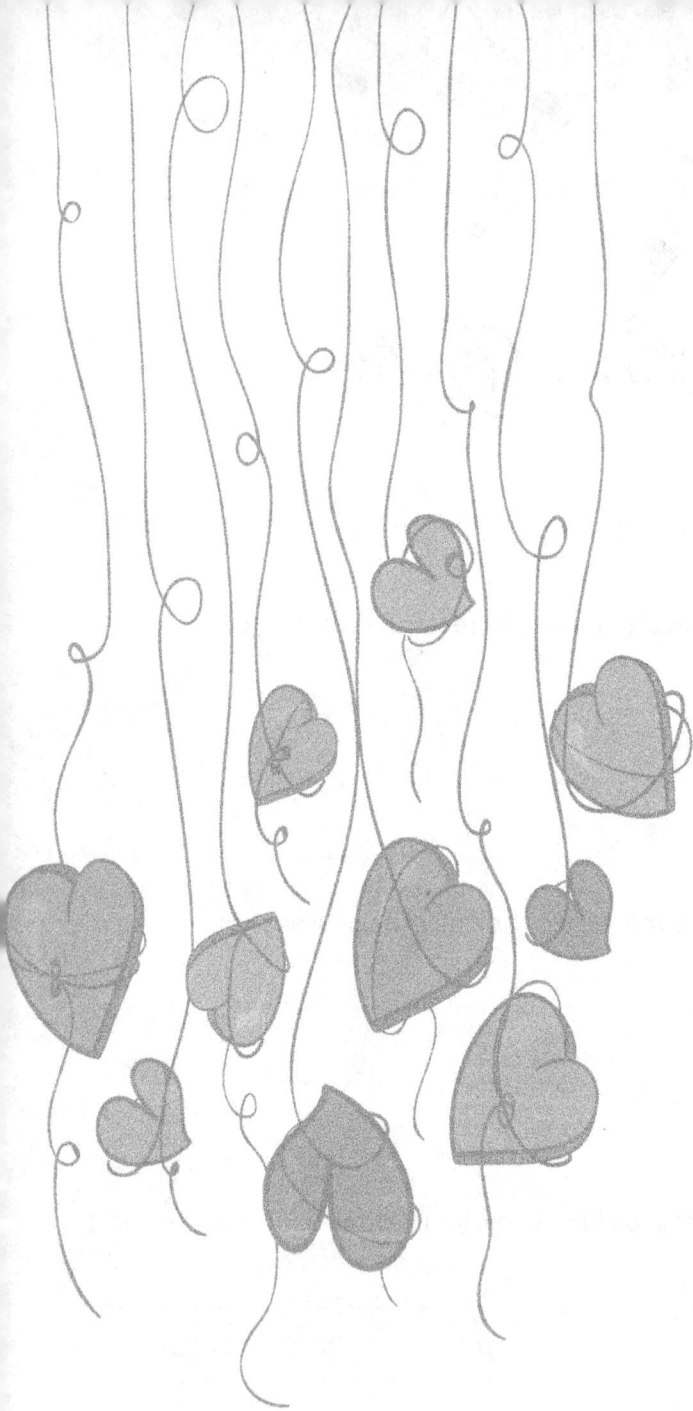

WEEK 43

Sun Sets, Love Rises

FOR THIS WEEK'S TIP, WE RETURN TO LUCIAN BLAKE'S APPROACH TO wooing. In the scene referenced in Week 39, he whisked his love-shy lady to the park for a sunset picnic. During this magical cinematic moment, both characters let down their guard and grow closer than either intended. Follow his example for Week 43 of *52 Love*: enchant your partner with a mesmerizing sunset.

Sharing a stunning sunset can slow your perception of time. As evening embraces the day, ease your minds. Relax your spirits. Give your brains the chance to recharge. Let peace permeate you and your partner while the golden rays warm you from the inside out. Watch shadows lengthen as the sun sinks below the horizon. Break from fretting over the past or worrying about the future. Untangle from the complexities life brings with the simplicity of nature's golden hour.

Make it an event. Bring snacks, a cooler for cold beverages, or a thermos for hot. Hold hands from your favorite foldout chairs or snuggle on a plush blanket and savor the time in each other's arms.

Entwined with your partner, witness the ever-changing beauty of the sky at dusk. Gaze into the vast, color-splashed horizon as the sun cuts across a sea of blue sky. Vibrant magentas swirl into deep ambers. Rich purples explode across nature's pink canvas. When the sky lights up in electric orange and takes your breath away, it's okay to snap a few photos, but stay present in this moment with your partner. Take advantage of the incredible show nature offers and luxuriate in the romantic backdrop for your time together.

Meditate on the miraculous as you connect with nature. When it comes to reminding you of what's important, never underestimate the power of awe. During the glorious grandeur of your sunset rendezvous, let the silent majesty of the planet's orbit put your relationship into perspective. Appreciate life and who you have in yours. As the sun kisses the horizon, embrace your partner and do the same.

After the splendor of the setting sun, stick around for romantic stargazing, or plan your dusk date before an expected meteor shower. Beneath a brilliant glittering sky, relive teenage fantasies by making out under the stars. Reflect on the increased bond between you and look forward to chasing golden sunsets into your golden years.

Love Bites

1. Are you more drawn to sunsets or sunrises? Why?

_____

_____

_____

2. Which colors do you most associate with a sunset?

_____

_____

_____

3. Both of you close your eyes and describe the sunset you just watched together. Which parts did you each enjoy most?

_____

_____

_____

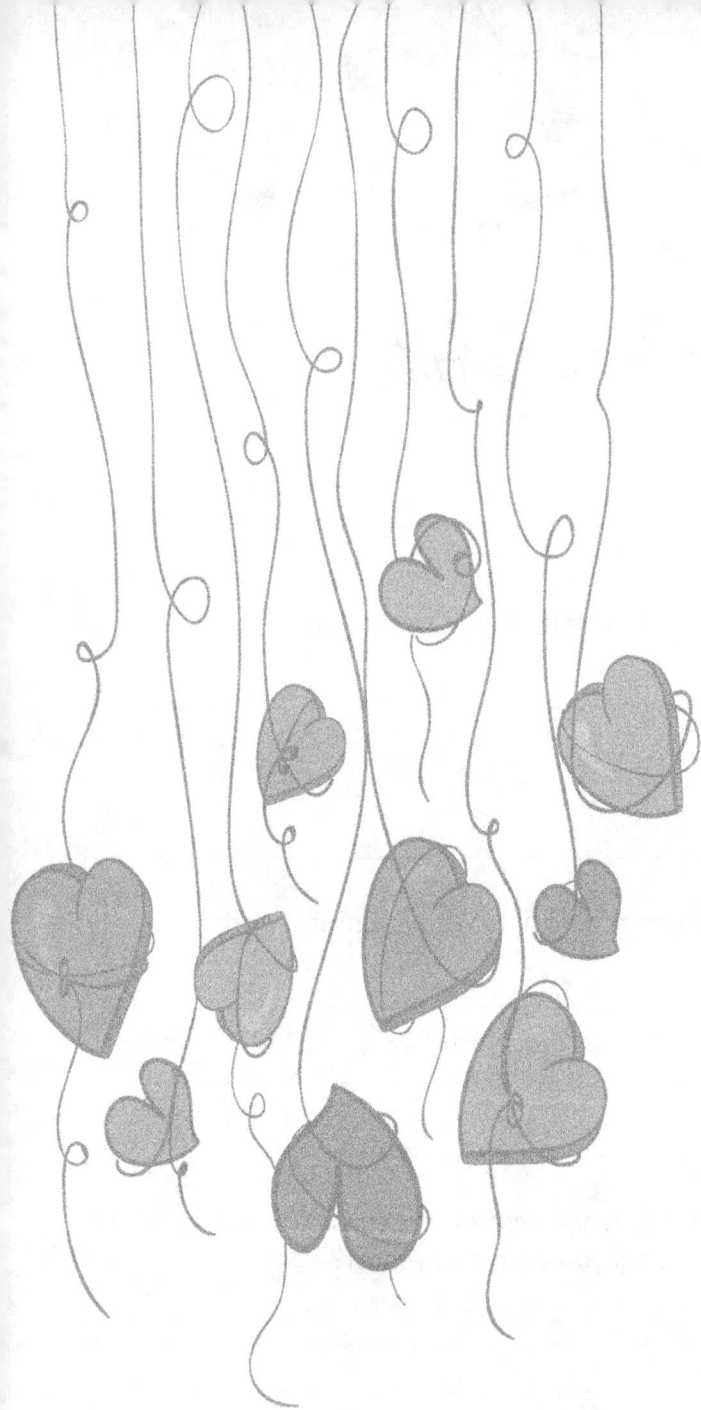

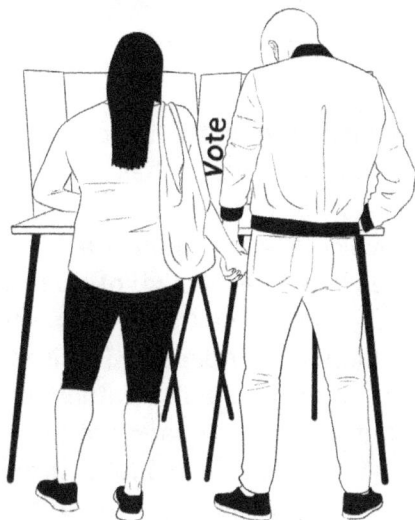

WEEK 44

The Ayes Have It

ELECTION SEASON MAY NOT BE THE MOST ROMANTIC TIME OF YEAR. NO Valentine's Day. No May flowers. No summer weddings. *52 Love* is about building long-term intimacy with your partner. In Week 4, I encouraged you to go for a walk. For Week 44, take that romantic stroll to the polls.

Reasons to vote go beyond determining the presidency. Election results impact your livelihood and that of future generations. Voting is your chance to stand up for issues that matter to you. You share the responsibility to influence change. Exercising your right to vote empowers you from within and emboldens you to actively make a difference.

As with other activities that feel good, your pleasure increases when you do it together. While placing your ballot demonstrates your investment in your future, voting together connects that long-term investment to your relationship. Align as a couple while you prepare for Election

Day. Review ballot questions and investigate candidates as a team. Some first-time voters may find the process challenging. Share what you discover to navigate the learning curve as a couple.

Voting together speaks to your solidarity as a couple and your commitment to each other first, irrespective of political party. Love transcends politics. Although you are a unit, your partnership consists of two individuals with independent opinions. This isn't the time to try and persuade your partner into voting in line with your choices. Hear each other's perspectives but leave the debating to the candidates.

Reshape the dialogue around civic duties. Discuss the importance of using your voice. Rejoice in your right to participate in democracy. Differing opinions can add a layer of passion to a relationship. So long as you and your partner share your ideas without demeaning each other, you can channel that passion into a post-vote celebration.

Make this social cohesion a date night. Dress for the occasion. Don patriotic colors for the voting booth. Proudly wear your "I voted" stickers and snap a selfie to preserve the memory. Then thank the volunteers, go home, pour champagne, and toast each other for performing your civic duties.

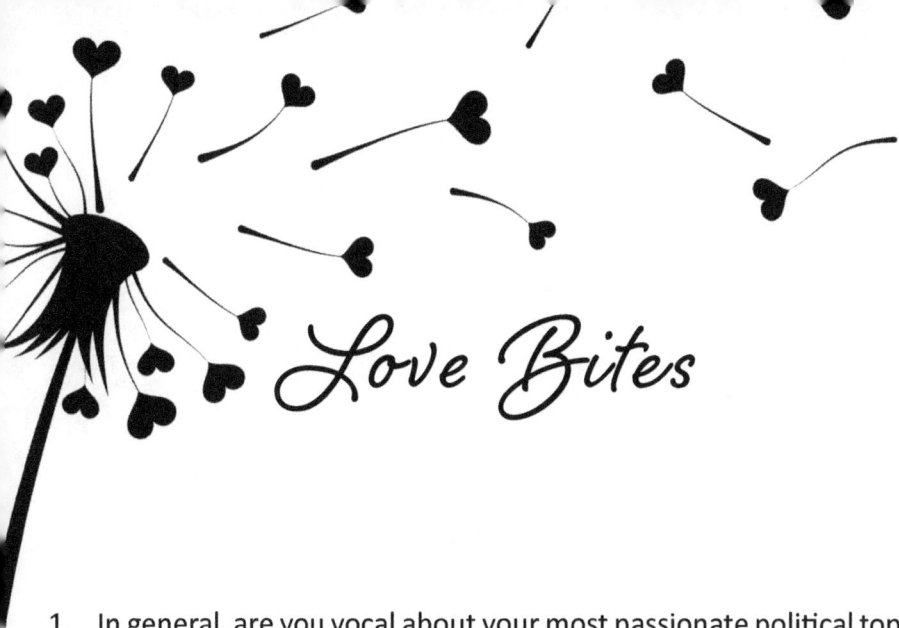

Love Bites

1. In general, are you vocal about your most passionate political topics, or do you prefer to keep your voting life private?

_____

_____

_____

2. Describe your first voting experience. What emotions do you recall?

_____

_____

_____

3. Whether campaigning for Class President or Treasurer for your local volunteer committee, share any experiences you have running for office. If none, what would motivate you to participate on this level?

_____

_____

_____

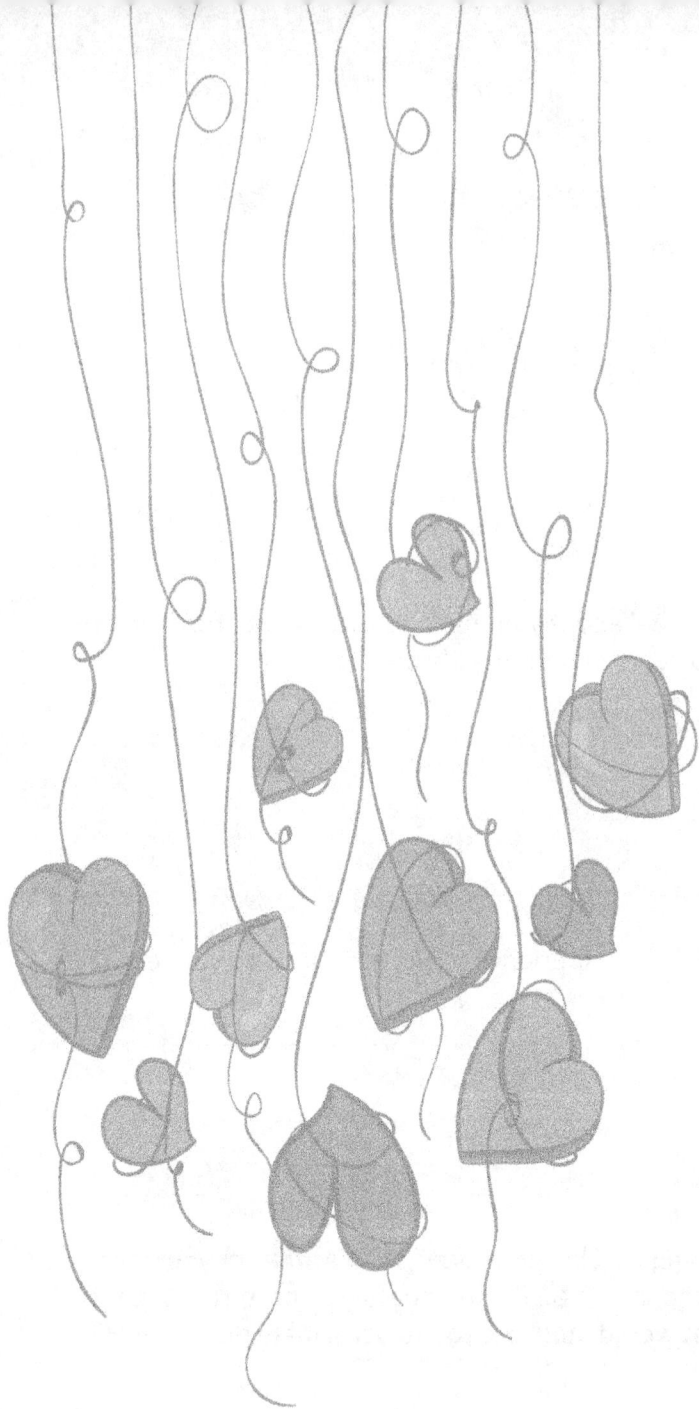

WEEK 45

Discover Your Lover's Lexicon

GOOD COMMUNICATION IS ESSENTIAL FOR A HEALTHY RELATIONSHIP, YET the way communication is received varies even when the information is the same. Take cats and dogs, for example. Tail movement conveys very different messages, both for sender and for receiver. The same applies to giving and receiving affection. When it comes to your relationship, avoid mistaking a warning twitch for a welcoming wag by learning which love language your partner speaks.

In 1992, counselor and speaker Dr. Gary Chapman penned *The Five Love Languages* to help couples determine their spouse's specific love styles. His studies found that expressing affection in the way your partner best receives it is the "secret to love that lasts." For Week 45 of *52 Love*, identify your partner's love language and apply your new knowledge toward greater intimacy.

In his book, Dr. Chapman details five categories: Acts of Service, Gifts, Physical Touch, Quality Time, and Words of Affirmation. When you focus on the ones less meaningful to your partner, the message may cross wires and miss its target. If you bring home an expensive gift when what your partner wants is to cuddle, you both feel unappreciated. Learning the love languages helps you communicate your affection as intended.

Expressing love in your partner's native tongue delivers the message loud and clear. It also shows you care enough to tailor your affections toward your partner's preferences. It's fair to dabble in all the love languages, but if you focus on your partner's favorites, the others will accentuate them like delicious side dishes to a hearty main course.

The best way to learn the love languages is to read the book. Full disclosure: while I stand behind the theory, the book was written with traditional spousal partnerships in mind. For a less extensive overview, review the Love Language website to get a grasp on the concept without the full heteronormative narrative or the sexist lens of its era. For the purpose of this week's topic, here's a brief definition of each.

Acts of Service – Whether you're assisting with chores or building a backyard gazebo, actions speak louder than words.

Gifts – Presents signify that your partner was on your mind when you weren't together. This may be as simple as an unexpected bouquet of flowers or as extravagant as a luxury watch. The thought really does count.

Physical Touch – Though lovemaking definitely falls into this category, touch doesn't have to be sexual. Frequent contact reassures your partner of your connection.

Quality Time – This is less about the amount of time and more about the level of focused engagement during your period of interaction.

Words of Affirmation – Verbally assert your affection. Use words that boost your partner's confidence.

After reviewing the definitions, analyze your partner's responses to affectionate gestures and categorize each one. If you notice a pattern, chances are that's your answer. It's possible for your partner to lean strongly toward two love languages. That's great. It gives you options.

Once you identify your lover's specialized vernacular, list the ways you usually communicate your affection. This will help you determine if your efforts are in the right areas. It may also highlight your own love language, as many show love in the way they like to receive it.

Better yet, take the website's couple's quiz together. Sharing answers will clear up uncertainty and solidify awareness of each other's preferences. Learning together offers another chance to explore the fun of Week 16. More importantly, your new proficiency will bloom into more skillful applications when expressing your love to one another. The message will root deeper and stick longer for a strong bond that endures beyond 52 weeks.

Love Bites

1. Before this week's exercise, what did you both know about the love languages?

_____

_____

_____

2. Have your love languages changed over time? How so?

_____

_____

_____

3. Do you tend to show love in the same language as you prefer to receive it, or are giving and receiving different for you?

_____

_____

_____

WEEK 46

Just Dessert

TONGUES SERVE AS ONE OF OUR MOST SENSUAL ORGANS. A TOOL OF THE mind as well as the body, our tongues encompass multiple simultaneous senses, both giving and receiving. With the right voice or word choice, flawless elocution whets many an appetite—as does the tactile satisfaction of a well-placed velvet stroke. A long languid lick also appeals to the eyes. And a burst of delectable flavors surging over taste buds sparks paradisiacal pleasure. Embrace this rapture by sharing a sweet treat with your partner. For Week 46 of *52 Love*, tantalize your tongues with dessert for two.

Food-play is akin to foreplay. The same sensations are triggered when you work them right. Desserts delight the palate and boost endorphins. That enjoyment multiplies when shared with a loved one. Sweet treats are festive and fun with lavish options to explore joint pleasures.

Often linked to increased sexual desire and prowess, honey serves as a natural aphrodisiac. Drizzle it over dessert and then each other. Suck droplets from your partner's fingers. Dab your pinkie in a gilded pool and glide it over his mouth. Lick the nectar from his honeyed lips as the prelude to a magnificent sticky kiss. Repeat with other body parts.

Add a sense of sinful pleasure by garnishing your chosen dessert with sliced apples or pomegranate seeds. No guilt involved. Only carmine antioxidants to nibble to your heart's desire. Choosing other fruits in vibrant colors will liven the scenery and add a sweet bouquet of aroma. Rest your partner's head on your lap and feed him grapes from the vine. Dip strawberries in whipped cream or melted chocolate, then slip the delectable tips between his lips. Lean in to share those flavor combinations with your tongue.

For a bonus sense of delayed gratification, prepare your dessert as a couple. It need not be difficult for you to enjoy the preparation process. Rejoice in the simplicity of boxed mixes and premade fillings or get fancy with extravagant make-together pastries. Preparing and decorating your treat as a couple fosters a sense of teamwork and closer intimacy, which extends the reward beyond the end goal. As always, working together toward this shared mutual pleasure builds anticipation toward the moment of culmination. Whether your dessert of choice is the magnum opus of your night or the prelude to a later crescendo, indulging in such rich decadence together will lead to a wealth of bliss that rewards more than your tongues.

Love Bites

1. What was your favorite childhood dessert?

_____

_____

_____

2. Try feeding each other dessert. How does this enhance the experience?

_____

_____

_____

3. What is your favorite treat to lick off of your partner?

_____

_____

_____

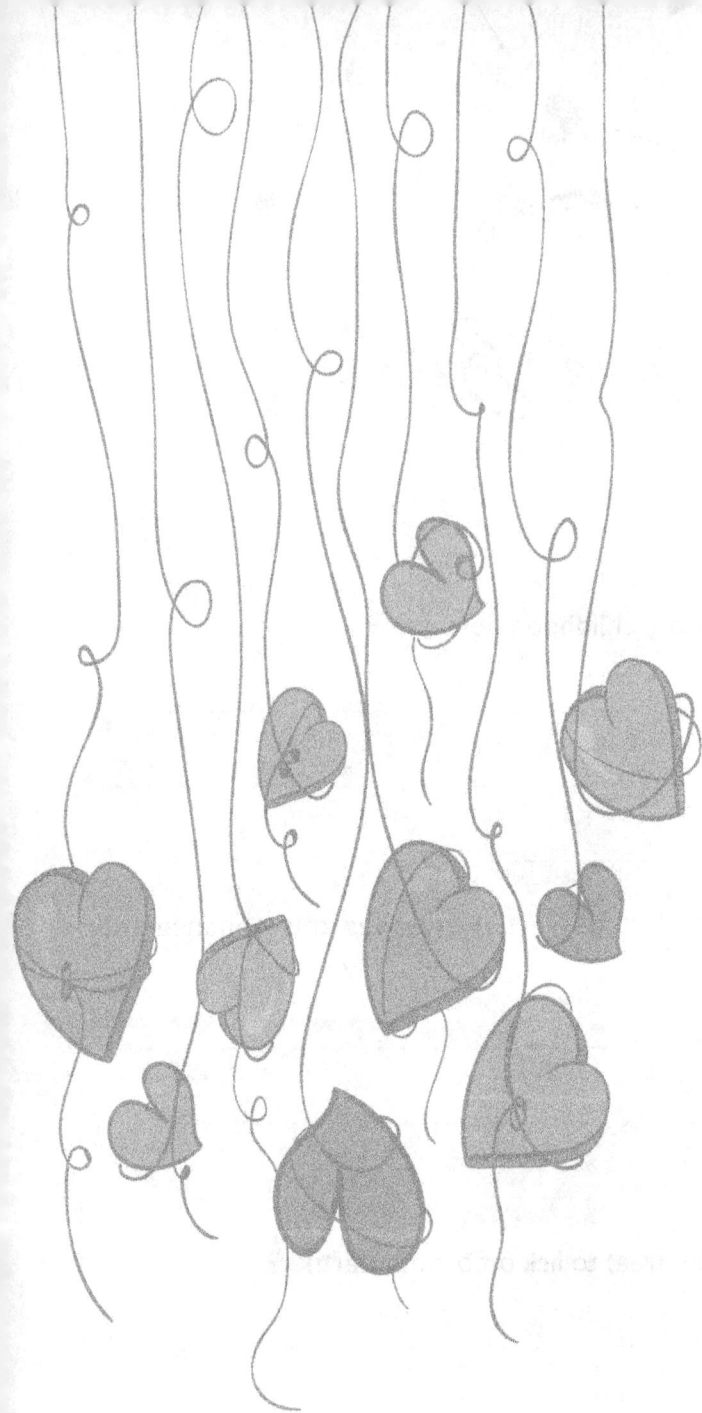

WEEK 47

Thanks from the Bottom of Your Heart

ACKNOWLEDGING OUR BLESSINGS LETS US RELEASE THE CHOKEHOLD ON old grudges and unmet desires to focus instead on the joys life has provided. When we stockpile our wins, they serve as reinforcements when reserves are low. For Week 47 of *52 Love*, take inventory of those blessings by harnessing the power of gratitude.

Research shows that communicating gratitude improves health and boosts happiness. Giving thanks is equally beneficial to your relationship. Connecting your spiritual gratitude as a couple can help you reach a level of tandem meditation that surpasses that of Week 18.

It's easier to voice thanks when you're already happy, but even if you're struggling, sharing this expression can lift your spirits and increase your bond. Painful circumstances can ease in favor of hope. And if you and your partner do start from a place of joy, your gratitude session can raise you to new happy heights.

Gratitude starts with the heart. Even though we use our minds to remember, a thankful attitude stems from affectionate recognition. How fitting that the person you've given your heart to shares this experience with you! Join hands with each other and speak your gratitudes as a connected unit.

Begin with the basics. Give thanks that your level of health allows you to participate in this exercise, for the minds that guide your thoughts, and for the bodies that keep you going. As anyone who's ever tread endless water or run a marathon can attest, it's possible for your body to quit on you. Remind your physical selves that you appreciate the effort that sustains your very being.

Next, look outside of yourselves to acknowledge the blessings around you. Voice appreciation for loved ones: families, friends, pets. Reflect on your recent opportunities and whatever work you're privileged to do. Give thanks for a warm place to sleep, food in your bellies, and other necessities. If you've required assistance in those areas, now's the time to speak gratitude for those who helped keep you afloat. If you've managed on your own, give thanks for that and for the abundance to help others.

Once you've recognized the blessings outside of your partner, shift your focus to one another. Often, the time and energy invested toward a successful relationship can go unnoticed. Spoken gratitude protects couples from the toxic effects of conflict and from the external stressors that can tear people apart. Your partnership means a built-in companion during troubling times and a cheerleader to celebrate successes. Share your appreciation for your partner's contribution to your life by exchanging the ways your life benefits from each other's presence.

Articulate why you love your partner, the ways she makes you feel appreciated, the things you've learned from her, and the times she made you smile. Then truly listen to how you benefit her, the blessings you've gifted, and the reasons she loves you.

Once each of you has spoken, maintain the connection within each other's arms. Embrace that state of peace and contentment. Bask in the glow of the blessings from your life together, the year you've shared, the moments you now preserve. Allow these reminders to flow through you as a dynamic vibrational experience that elevates your awareness of your past blessings and opens you to a more fulfilling future together.

Love Bites

1. Did you grow up in a household of gratitude? How did that shape who you are today?

_____

_____

_____

2. Hold hands. How does physical contact enhance this week's lesson?

_____

_____

_____

3. Write down the blessings you discussed as battle reinforcements for trying times.

_____

_____

_____

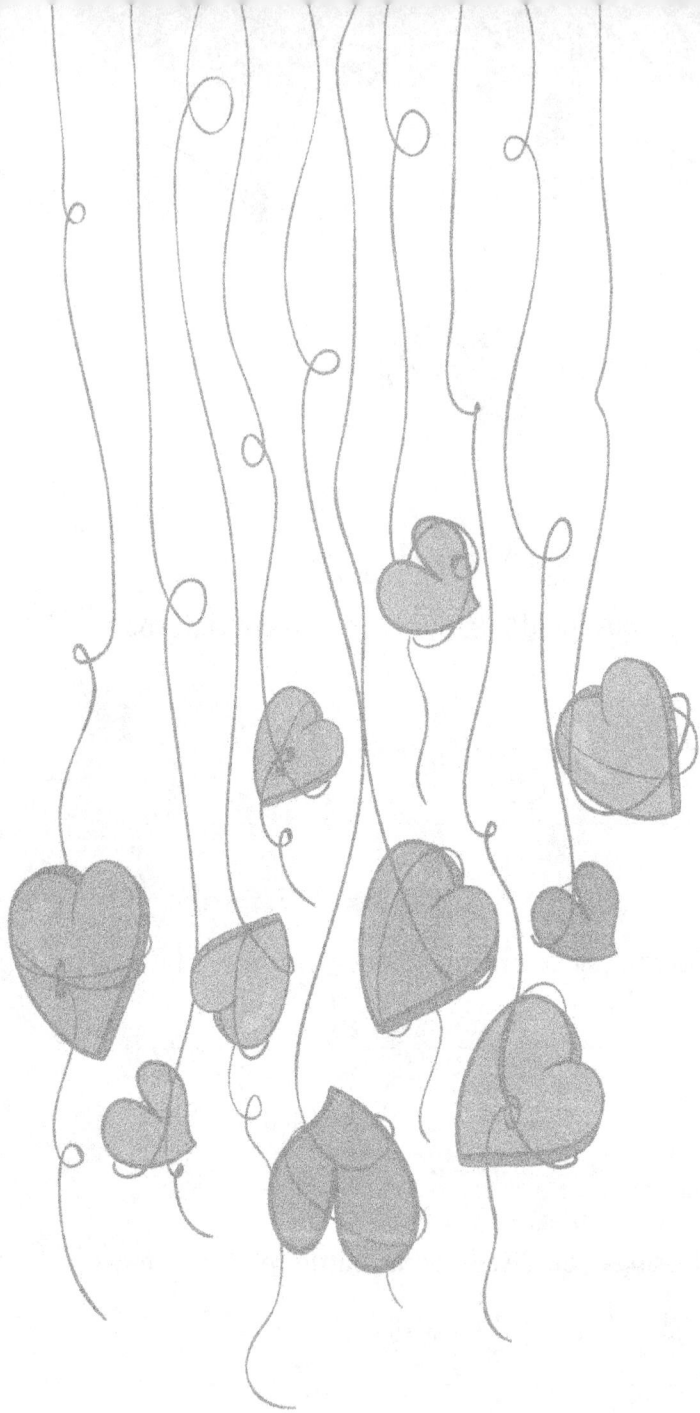

WEEK 48

Ballroom Bliss

DANCING BRINGS US TOGETHER, NOT JUST IN THE BODY BUT IN THE MIND and spirit. In previous weeks, we discussed the joy of dancing with your partner and the value of learning new skills together. For Week 48 of *52 Love*, sweep your partner off his feet with a combination of both. Sign up for ballroom dance instruction.

Dancing releases endorphins. Elevated moods boost the immune system by relieving stress and thwarting depression. As with many forms of exercise, dancing enhances cardiovascular health, increases circulation, burns calories, and improves stamina.

Organized ballroom instruction heightens cognitive performance and challenges your brain. By incorporating movements on several planes of motion and from many directions, the structured choreography improves strength, balance, and flexibility. Unlike when simply exercising at the same time or engaging in competitive sport, you and your partner are truly working out together. Instead of rivaling one another, you are a team of two—joined, face to face, whirling and twirling toward the same goal.

If your knowledge of ballroom dancing is limited to period films, you may have unrealistic expectations. This skill requires practice even for the most graceful novice. You will work hard, you will make mistakes, and you will overcome them together. Have plenty of water on hand and towels to dab each other between dances.

Choosing what to wear is an essential step toward success. Select unrestricted clothing that allows you to move. Comfort is best. This is equally important for your shoes. Even if you or your partner are experienced with five-inch stilettos, begin with a low heel to prevent injury. Eventually, you can add fancy clothes or even cosplay to the mix to create an entire experience.

Partner dancers must learn to think and move in sync by communicating with non-verbal cues. Start with basic routines so that you can rehearse patterns as a couple. Give each other time to master new concepts without rushing. For beginning dancers who find it intimidating to prance their two left feet in front of others, try an online option. Many studios provide lessons through live or recorded instructional videos. Whether you opt for online or in-person classes, line up a series of date nights to practice together.

Once familiar with the basic concepts, you and your partner can synchronize with less effort. Eventually, the two of you will move as a single unit. Embracing the sensuality of the dance, your bodies will take over, leaving your minds to focus on each other. Concentrate on your partner's proximity, his body heat, and his touch.

Wrapped in each other's arms, shake off the outside world, lock eyes, and let the music pulse through you as your bodies speak to one another, angling, shifting, connecting through a shared rhythm. Find that special zone where all else disappears, leaving you and your dance partner as the only two in the room—a concept shown brilliantly in the 2005 *Pride & Prejudice*.

Couples dance lessons can lead to a more satisfying physical relationship. The joint exhilaration of nailing a quick-quick-slow combination can lead to tandem celebrations off the dance floor. At its core, ballroom dance fosters an appreciation for synchronized, heart-racing, hip-thrusting action. When mastered, it provokes two bodies in close proximity into meeting each other's rhythm in the aim of a shared climax. What a wonderful way to keep the flame burning.

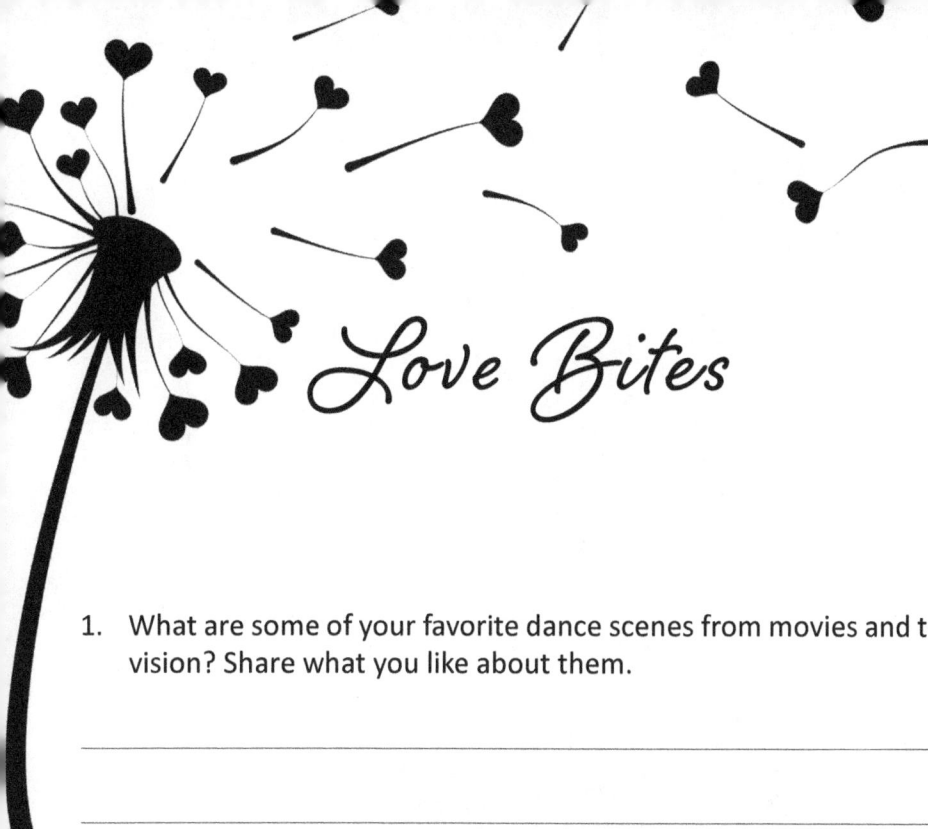

Love Bites

1. What are some of your favorite dance scenes from movies and television? Share what you like about them.

_____

_____

_____

2. Which element of taking ballroom dance lessons was the most intimidating? Which part was the most fun?

_____

_____

_____

3. If you could learn any style of dance, what would you choose? Why?

_____

_____

_____

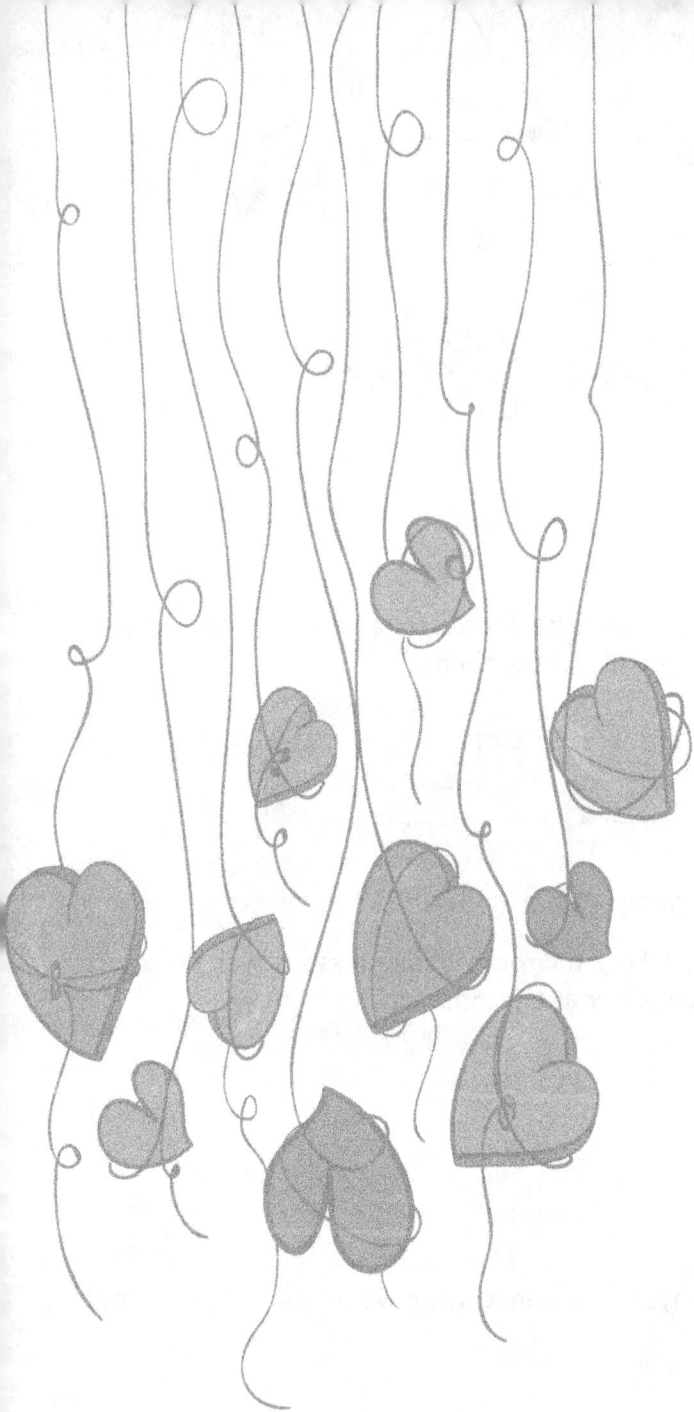

WEEK 49

Bare Necessities

HUGGING CREATES A SENSE OF WELL-BEING AND HAPPINESS. PUT SIMPLY, it feels good. At a large party, especially one where you know few people, a friendly hug at arrival eases anxiety and makes you feel welcome. Even a stranger's embrace envelops you in comfort, releasing the same type of endorphins the body dispenses after a good workout. You'll find the ultimate solace, however, wrapped in the arms of someone you love. This soothing sensation is improved with the removal of clothes. For Week 49 of *52 Love*, cuddle naked with your partner.

Skin-on-skin contact does more than fuel intimacy. Naked cuddling is good for your health. Touch relieves pain, both physical and emotional. Beyond easing the discomforts of trauma, a loving caress reallocates the focus of your nerves from the negative sensation to the pleasurable touch. Skin-to-skin contact releases oxytocin, which reduces pain levels, lowers blood pressure, aids in healing, and decreases the production of cortisol, giving your immunity levels a boost.

Nude snuggling is linked to improved relational satisfaction. Cradling your partner in your arms is a non-verbal way to communicate her importance to you. It whispers the sweet words some find uncomfortable voicing. "I treasure you. I'm here for you. I want you close to me."

Many people struggle with body dysmorphia. That sense of vulnerability is countered by a partner's loving embrace. Unguarded, yet secure in each other's arms, baring yourself to your partner builds trust. Spending more time naked together will help you both grow more comfortable in your own skins. As your comfort with your bodies increases, so does your self-esteem and confidence.

You may have guessed that nude snuggling can lead to other naked activities. Oxytocin is also considered the love hormone. Access to skin naturally encourages more physical intimacy. Cuddling leads to canoodling. And canoodling releases dopamine, which increases sexual desire. Yet the oxytocin released means you are just as likely to fall asleep as you are to have sex. Whether you start your snuggle as precursor to a refreshing nap, as foreplay, or as a post-coital indulgence, naked cuddling affirms your emotional bond.

Look for ways to incorporate snuggling into your days and nights. Stand and hold one another or cozy up on a cushy couch. Spoon together, nestle your head to your partner's chest, lightly touch or massage each other. *The Cuddle Sutra* by Rob Grader offers additional suggestions. Among them, I recommend Melting Butter, Breakfast in Bed, and the full-frontal classic Forking.

If you and your partner cuddle naked in the morning, you can start your day warding off stress, anxiety, high blood pressure, and even the common cold without having to leave your bed. As you embrace the full-body contact of inviting skin, you'll feel more physically and psychologically connected with your snuggle bunny.

Love Bites

1. How did hugs play a role in your upbringing? How did that shape your relationship with hugging as an adult?

_____

_____

_____

2. Did you grow up with a family that was comfortable being naked around one another? How has that translated to your level of comfort with casual nudity in your home?

_____

_____

_____

3. Now that you know naked cuddling is good for your health, how often will you incorporate it into your relationship?

_____

_____

_____

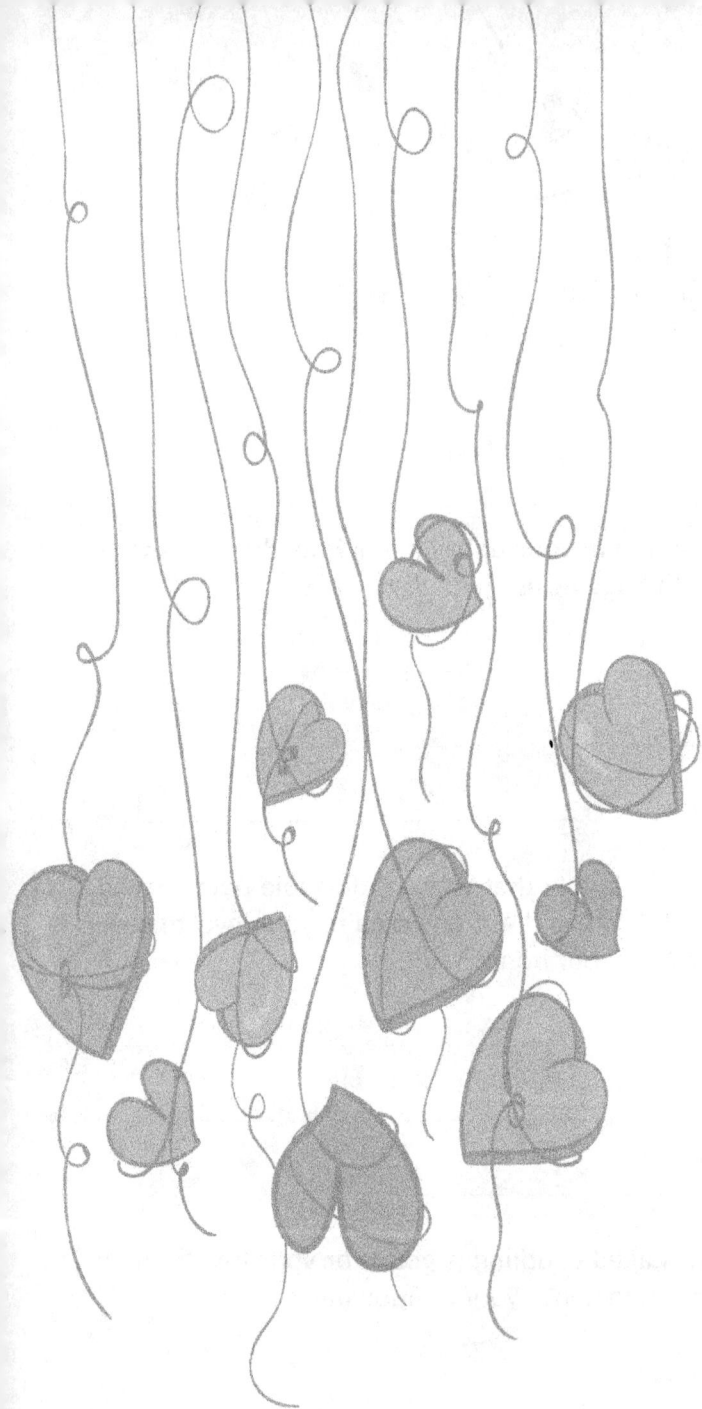

WEEK 50

Tactical Romantics

NEW YEAR'S DAY REPRESENTS A CLEAN SLATE, BUT WAITING UNTIL THE last minute to write resolutions means less time to consider your commitments and true goals. As we celebrate the holiday season and approach the end of this historic year, take a moment with your partner to plan upcoming resolutions.

Making New Year's resolutions together energizes your partnership by communicating that you have plans for the future, and those plans include each other. And let's be honest—resolutions tend to get a bad rap because people rarely follow through with them. Setting goals with your partner deepens accountability. Preparing your lists together will help you inspire each other to keep going when your goals challenge you in the new year.

As you work together, define and discuss your own individual goals. Being emotionally honest involves making yourself vulnerable. Foster a closer bond as you confess perceived shortcomings and wishes for self-improvement. Confide your dreams and secret desires for what you'll accomplish next year. Listen with interest as your partner shares the same. Support those goals, even if they feel unrealistic to you. Be the voice of encouragement.

Help one another identify the best steps to accomplish these resolutions. Brainstorm ideas. Which obstacles can you help each other overcome? Determine what each of you is willing to contribute to the achievement of those personal goals. Commit to supporting each other when persisting gets tough.

Now that you've assisted each other, cultivate your connection by creating one or two couple's goals together. Make intimacy a priority in the new year and decide which strategies you'll use to nourish your relationship.

Record your resolutions and plan to re-examine them each month. Expect that there will be speed bumps and divots on your journeys. Outline steps to recover from expected challenges. Make a date of review night. Practice last week's clothing-optional cuddles. Cut off outside distractions and cozy up to evaluate your progress.

If nothing else, your monthly review will serve as one more commitment in quality time and a reminder of what you mean to each other. And because you're compiling your lists now, when the fireworks ignite, your midnight kiss will launch the new year with more than a heartfelt promise in the moment. You'll have a blueprint for the best year of your relationship.

Love Bites

1. Are you goal-oriented by nature?

_____

_____

_____

2. Which of the goals you set feels the most challenging? What can you do to support each other through those challenges?

_____

_____

_____

3. After completing this exercise, do you feel prepared for the year? If not, what can you do to change that?

_____

_____

_____

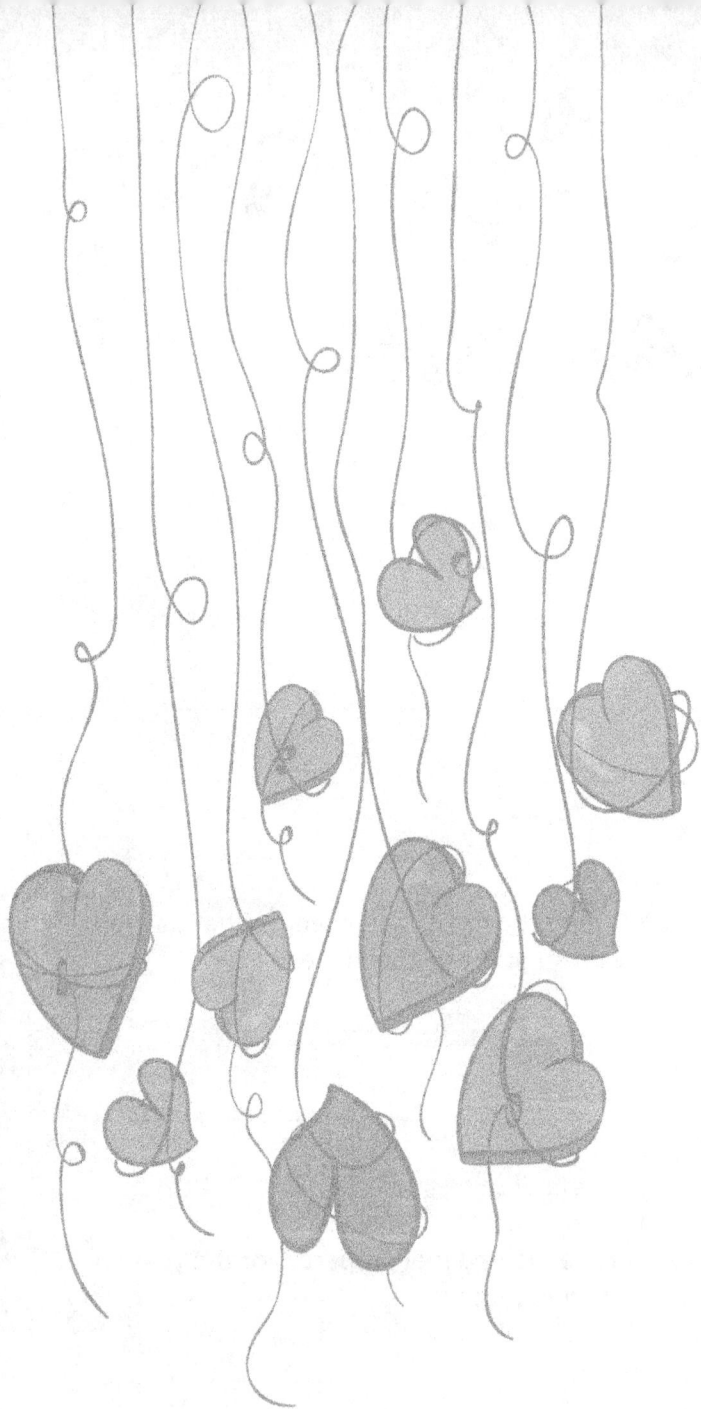

WEEK 51

Double Bubbles

DECK THE HALLS WITH DECEMBER MADNESS. NO MATTER WHAT YOU celebrate this time of year, festivities flurry in a winter whirlwind. As we approach the end of the month, take some time to wash away the stress that often accompanies these activities by getting wet, hot, and steamy with your partner. For Week 51 of *52 Love*, escape the hustle and bustle of the holiday season with a bubble bath for two.

Unwinding with a hot bath soothes stress while kindling intimacy. With a few careful details, you and your partner can relax together in style. It's okay if you aren't blessed with a walk-in tub or your bath isn't big enough for two. If you find your tub too snug for your comfort, try a whirlpool Jacuzzi or spa. Or take turns pampering each other from the edge of the tub, then rinse together in the shower.

First, set the stage. Create a cozy, intimate space as the perfect set-ting for your romantic soak. Whether hot tub or bathtub, decorative candles around the rim and throughout the room help create a boundary between you and the rest of the world. Placing candles in front of a mirror offers the illusion of more candles. Magnify the flickering candlelight by arranging groups on reflective chrome and silver surfaces. Augment the magical glow with twinkle lights.

Enhance the ambiance by indulging more of your senses. Scatter rose petals along the path leading to your spa or bathtub, then sprinkle some on top of the water for a romantic and fragrant effect. Adding essential oils and bath salts to the water introduces aromatherapy to your experience. Pleasant scents can relax or invigorate, depending on your selection.

Music enchants the soul. Smooth jazz. Sultry blues. Seductive R&B. Make a playlist to affect the desired mood, be it escape, romantic bliss, provocative suggestion, or some combination.

If using a traditional tub, leave room to accommodate your bodies without spilling onto the floor. Start with the temperature a little hotter than comfortable. Use your elbow to test the water. While you wait for it to cool, offer a striptease or undress your partner.

Once you both submerge in your frothy tub, a couple's bath allows ample opportunity to incorporate many of the year's *52 Love* tips. Listen during a peaceful heart-to-heart. Read aloud from a favorite book. Wash your sweetie's hair. Get lost in each other's eyes.

Fully enjoy your cocoon for two. If in a Jacuzzi, snuggle near the jets. If in a bathtub, offer your partner a therapeutic scrub with an exfoliating glove, mitt, or loofah sponge. With either locale, use the intimate setting to massage away your lover's tension in shoulders, neck, head, legs, hands, and feet. Explore erogenous zones. Stimulate circulation. Edible scrubs exfoliate and introduce another sense to the mix. Lick the excess from your fingertips. Tease your partner with underwater foreplay, then tempt with a show, gliding your hands over your smooth, glistening skin.

When you reach your limit of fun in the tub, prolong the experience with generous afterbath care. Have fluffy towels or bathrobes warmed and ready. Caress your partner with body butter, rich lotion, or almond oil to hold in the moisture. To hydrate from within, toast your rejuvenating interlude with champagne or sparkling cider.

End the night snuggling by the fireplace or cuddle naked in the clean sheets of a freshly made bed. From bubbles to bubbly, you'll find a hot bath for two the perfect festivity to warm winter days and heat holiday nights.

Love Bites

1. After a hot bath, are you the type of person who falls fast asleep, or are you stimulated from bathing?

_____

_____

_____

2. What were some other *52 Love* Tips that you incorporated during this week's tip? What could you incorporate next time?

_____

_____

_____

3. Other than the heat of the water, what are some of the senses you recall from this experience?

_____

_____

_____

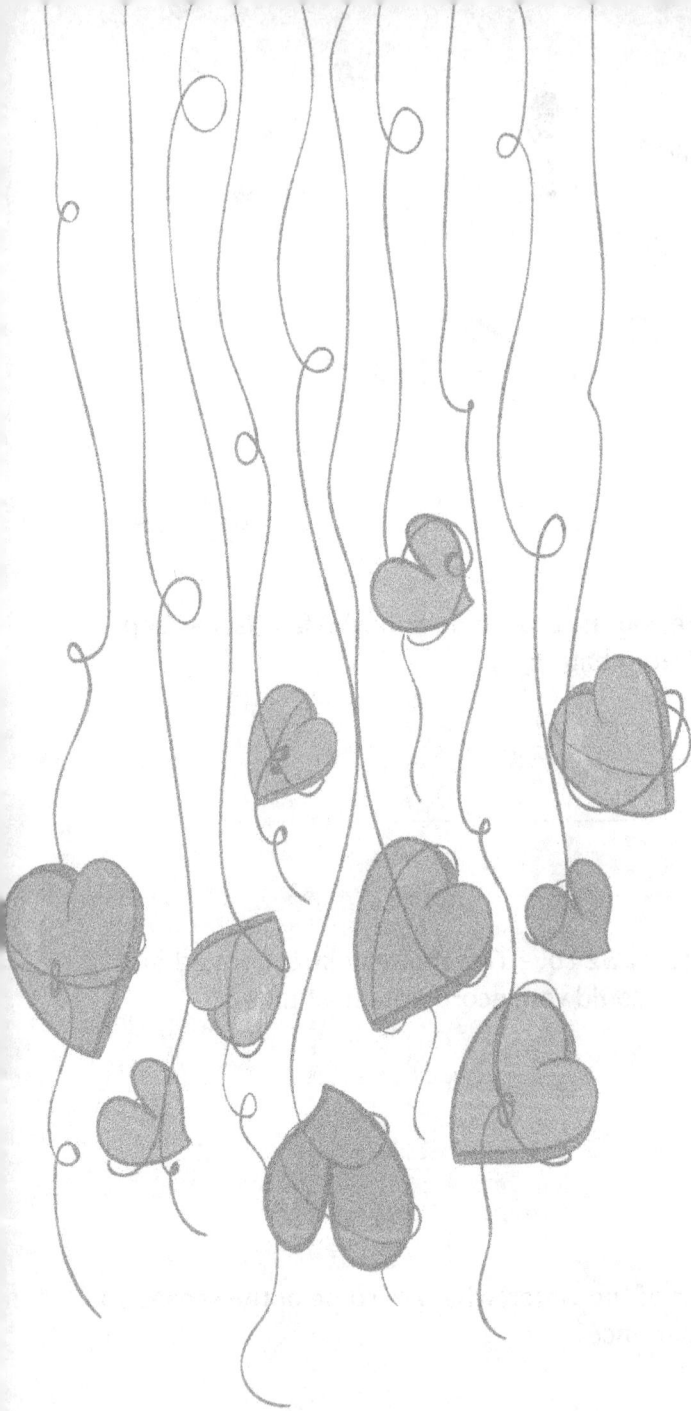

WEEK 52

Deck Your Halls

NEW YEAR'S REPRESENTS A TIME TO COMMEMORATE THE OLD AND welcome the new, a chance for merry revelry and final indulgences before the clock resets. The final holiday of the year is often synonymous with wild ventures, massive gatherings, and grand extravagances, most of which lack the intimacy practiced during this series. Keep the excitement without the crowds and cover charges. For the *52 Love* finale, bid farewell to the last twelve months with an at-home New Year's celebration for two.

You don't have to live in Vegas to catch the New Year's party craze. Tidy your home as if you're hosting friends. Decorate with glitz and glamour galore. Depending on your preferred atmosphere, dim lamps and line walls with twinkling holiday bulbs or hang a disco ball from the ceiling so it can twirl and reflect a multitude of colorful lights. Sprinkle sparkling trinkets, festive flowers, and colorful candles throughout your home. Dress in your fanciest digs or treat yourself to new spangly out-fits befitting the holiday. Whether confetti and crowns or poppers and party hats, your accessories highlight the experience.

Use all the space on a dance floor for two. Create a playlist of your favorite party music and dance jams. When your twinkle toes need a break, try couples karaoke with songs that require dual melodies. Belt your favorite tracks like it's the last time you'll hear them this year. With the money you save by staying home, splurge on takeout from an upscale restaurant. Pull out the fine china and include a lavish dessert.

If you're a fan of the bar scene, get in the spirit with spirits. Stock up on your favorite beers, wines, liquors, and liqueurs. Use the evening to practice your mixing skills. Prepare holiday libations to toast the new year. If you're feeling particularly festive, leave a different set of cocktails (or mocktails) in every room of the house for a personalized New Year's Eve bar crawl. You won't have to wait in line for an overpriced drink, and you don't need to worry about driving home.

If a relaxing celebration is more your style, order in, curl up together, and exchange quiet reflections. Read your couples journal together. Review your goals. Make a time capsule with your partner that com-memorates your favorite books, movies, songs, podcasts, and TV shows from the last twelve months. Include tokens from the special times you've shared throughout the year.

Play board games. Or video games. Or make up your own game, like no lip-to-lip-contact until midnight, then plant kisses every place else on your partner. Start a new tradition, such as an edible countdown: treats and snacks to nibble at each hour approaching midnight. At the final hour, feed each other twelve grapes for good luck to bring prosperity in the new year.

Chill your favorite bubbly by the bedside and toast the New Year from between the sheets. Watch marathon movies. Stack the queue with your favorite holiday films or the entire Marvel Cinematic experience.

Whether you party hard or settle in for some low key cuddle time, set an alarm to ensure you catch the countdown to your midnight kiss. Celebrate the blessings and joyful moments of this year as well as the hopeful anticipation of what's to come for you and your partner. Much like the year, this night is for the two of you. Enjoy it to its fullest. Cheers!

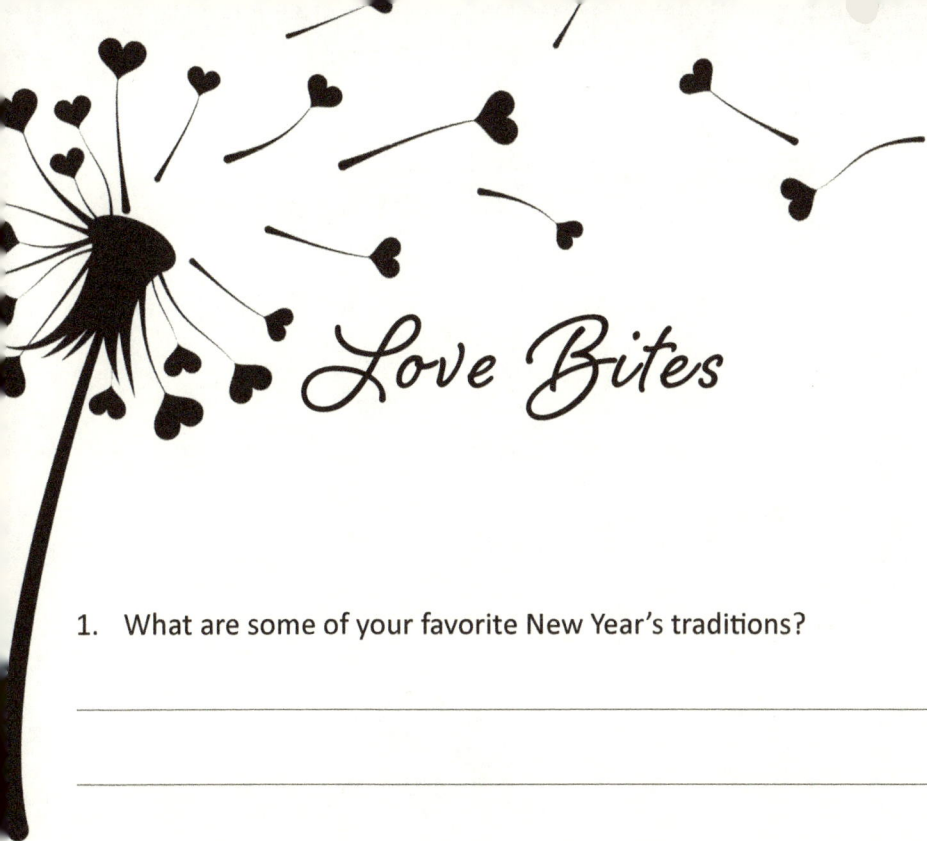

Love Bites

1. What are some of your favorite New Year's traditions?

   _____

   _____

   _____

2. What are you most looking forward to in the new year?

   _____

   _____

   _____

3. Reflect on your *52 Love* experience. What were some of your favorites this year? Which ones do you think you will try again next year?

   _____

   _____

   _____

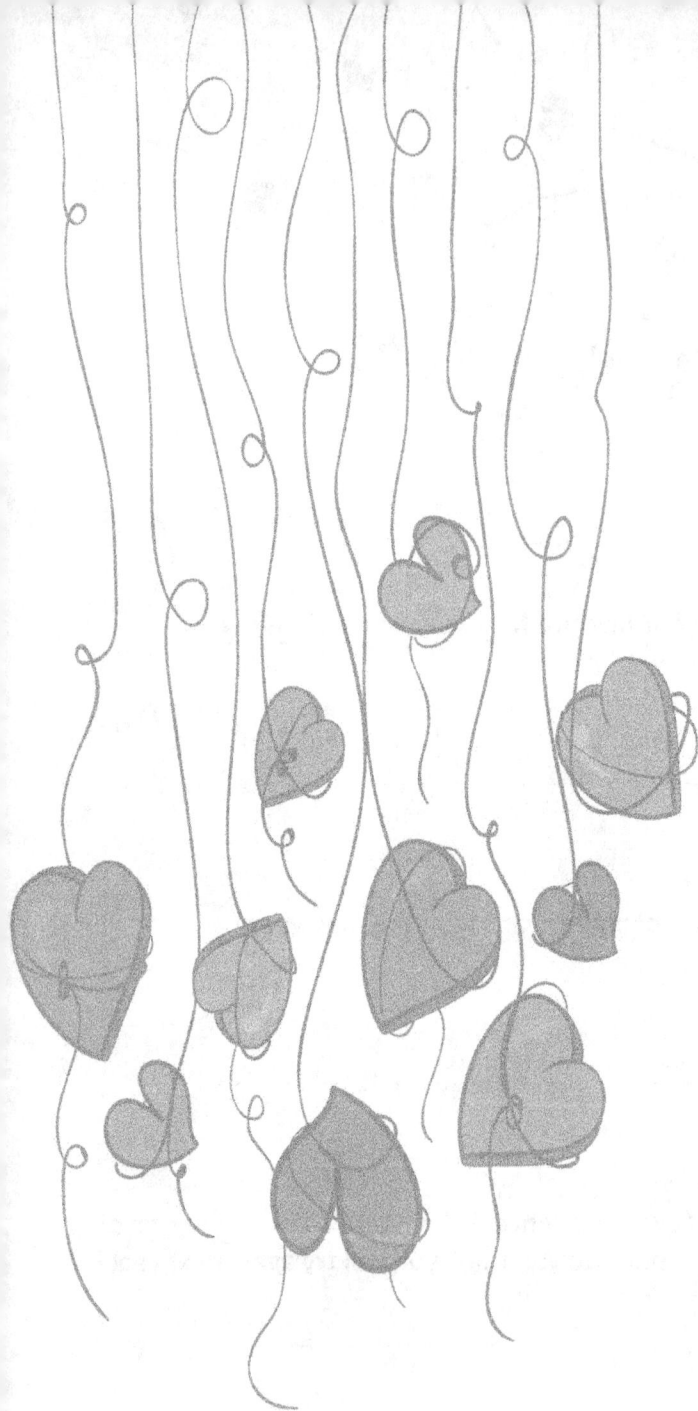

AUTHOR BIO

TONYA TODD IS INVESTED IN OWN VOICES WRITING AND DIVERSE representation in both the literary and cinematic worlds she inhabits. During her four years on the board of Henderson Writers Group, Tonya spearheaded education for authors at all levels. Her involvement in the literary, theatre, and filmmaking communities provides a platform to champion marginalized artists and contributes toward an environment that embraces a variety of voices. In her role as host of *The 52 Love Podcast*, she interviewed a myriad of creatives dedicated to celebrating love and art in all its forms. Her writing explores the infinite hues of what drives us all: relationships and desires.

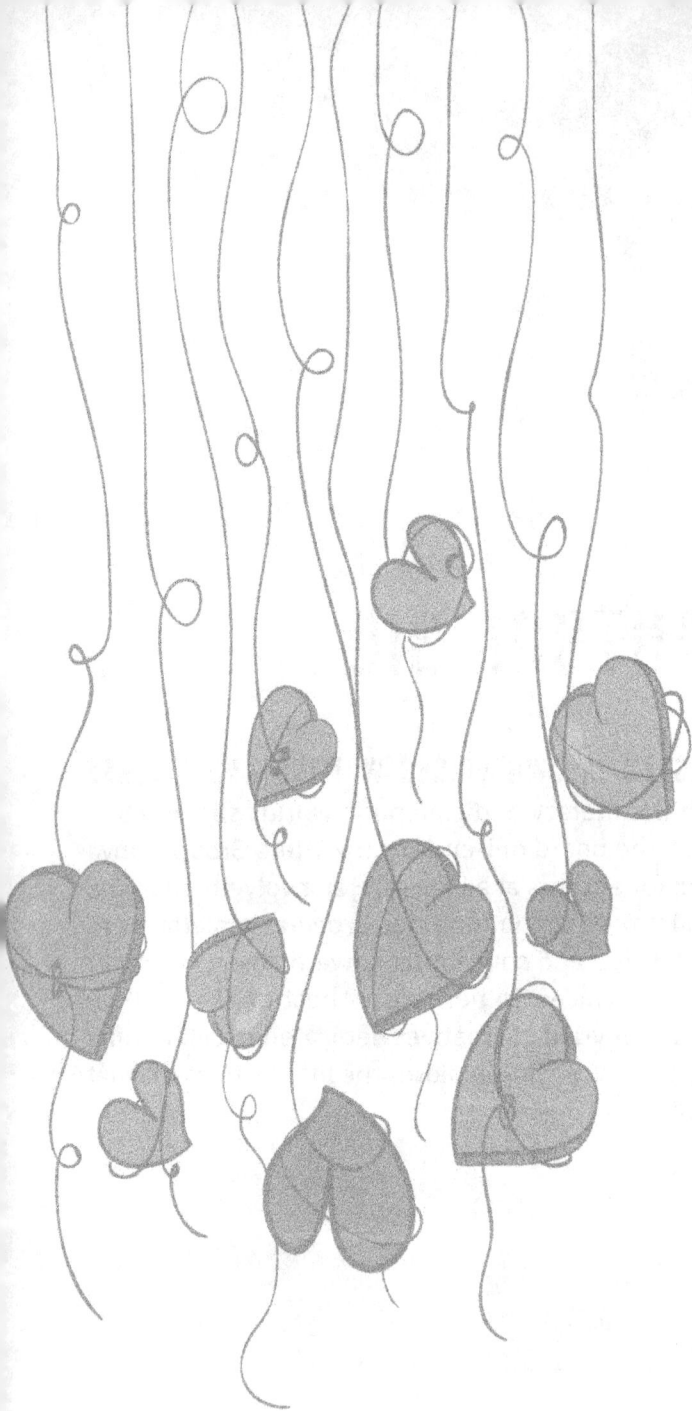

THANK YOU

THANK YOU FOR EMBARKING ON THE 52 LOVE JOURNEY WITH ME. NOW that you've read the how-to, see how your favorite characters navigate these ideas in four installments of *52 Love: A Year of Romance.* Each volume in the series will showcase thirteen authors sharing short stories that feature the love lessons in this book. Read how the first thirteen intimacy tips play out in Volume One, release coming soon, if not already at your favorite book stores.

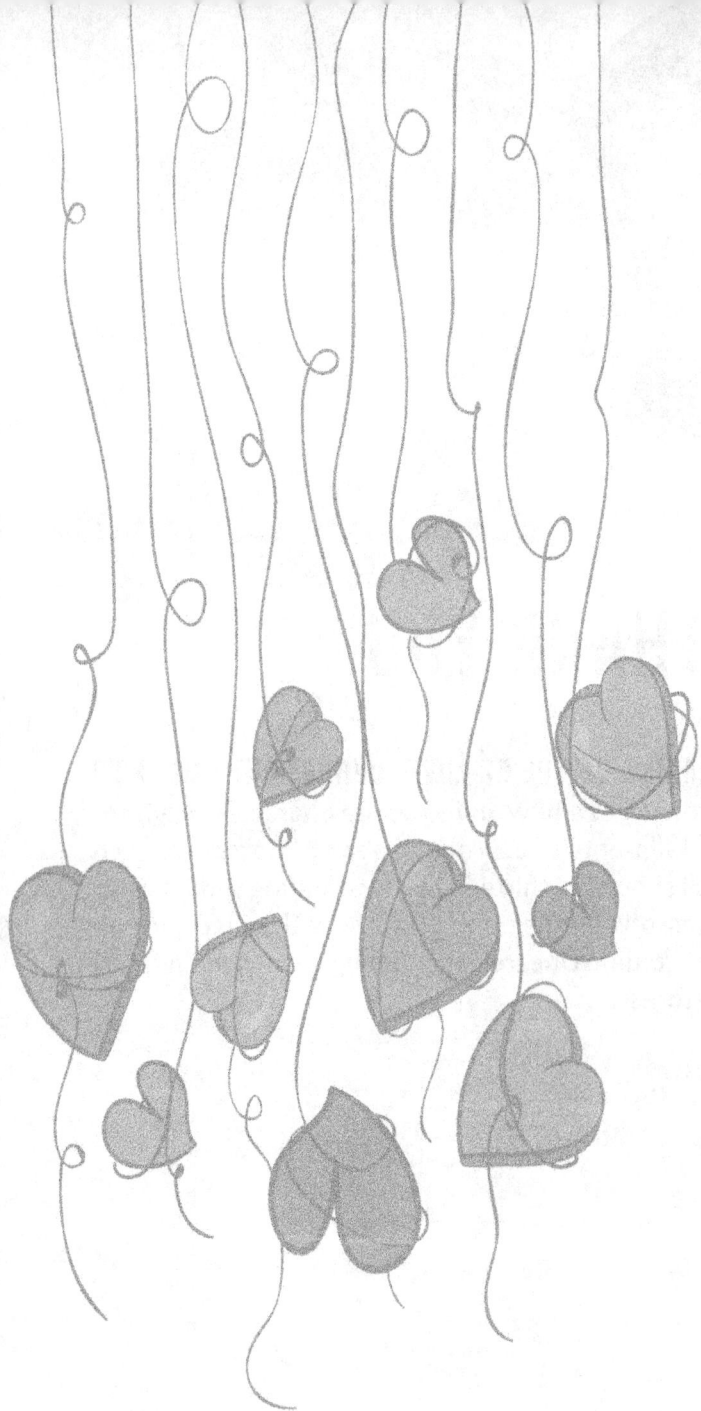

ACKNOWLEDGMENTS

THERE ARE MANY I WISH TO THANK FOR SUPPORTING ME ON THE PATH TO publishing this book. As such, I extend the following gratitudes:

To my mother for believing I can do anything.

To Diamond, Michael, and James for proving that it's true.

To Charles, Jerry, and Kris—As the first to hear my dreams, you could have quashed them. Instead, you offered to be early readers of my messy drafts.

To Charlie, Erica, and Stacey for taking my career seriously.

To Terri Maue and Ron Fink for holding me accountable to my goal and reading those initial weekly blog posts. Our Sunday sessions were a Godsend.

To Amy Collins for believing in this project before others did. We may not have found a home for *52 Love* together, but it would still be an orphan without your influence in my journey.

To 4 Horsemen Publications for their willingness to see potential outside the realm of their usual saddles.

To Mel Walker for pushing me to strive beyond my initial vision.

To Mike Burton for advising me on *The 52 Love Podcast*, designing my logo, and promoting my work at every opportunity.

To my publicist Bruce Wawrzyniak for finding creative ways to boost my career and for introducing me to Mike.

To the *And I Thought Ladies*, Jade and Wilnona, for fanning my flames, cheering me on, and for introducing me to Bruce.

To all of *The 52 Love Podcast* guests who tried the tips, shared their experiences, and in doing so, taught me more about using Love as a Verb.

To Gregory Kompes for reminding me to keep writing through roadblocks, setbacks, and depression. I may have banked all my potential for success in one basket had it not been for your shared wisdom.

To Henderson Writers Group for giving me a place to find my voice.

To The Writer Workshop for ensuring that voice was not only polished but inclusive.

To Amanda Skenandore, Ilanit Moskal, Oksana Marafioti, and Wendy Wimmer, the covenant of our sisterhood taught me the power of female friendships.

To my precious group of superfans. One day I hope to earn the support you give so generously.

And, most of all, to God for bringing these people into my life.

BOOK CLUB QUESTIONS

1. What was the intent or objective of this book? What do you feel was the author's purpose in writing it?

2. Did the book's contents fit with the book's cover?

3. What do you think of the book's title? Does it capture the essence of the book's contents? What other title might you choose?

4. How did you react to the author's writing style? Was it an easy read, or did you have to push through in order to finish?

5. What kind of language does the author use? Is it objective and dispassionate? Or passionate and earnest? Does the language help or undercut the author's premise?

6. Are the author's recommendations concrete, sensible, doable?

7. Talk about specific tips that struck you as significant. What was the most surprising tip in the book? Which tips were most memorable?

8. What have you learned after reading this book?

9. What challenged, changed, or confirmed what you already knew?

10. What feelings did this book evoke for you?

11. If you could ask the author one follow-up question, what would it be?

12. Have you ever read a book similar to this one? What makes this book different?

13. Would you want to reread this book? Why or why not?

14. In what situations would you recommend this book to your friends and family?

Discover more at
4HorsemenPublications.com

10% off using HORSEMEN10

www.ingramcontent.com/pod-product-compliance
Lightning Source LLC
Chambersburg PA
CBHW022050020426
42335CB00012B/623